The Ganja Godfather

The Untold Story of NYC's Weed Kingpin

Toby Rogers

Published by:
Trine Day LLC
PO Box 577
Walterville, OR 97489
1-800-556-2012
www.TrineDay.com
publisher@TrineDay.net

Library of Congress Control Number: 2014958809

Rogers, Toby
The Ganja Godfather: The Untold Story of NYC's Weed Kingpin—1st ed.
p. cm.
Epud (ISBN-13) 978-1-937584-96-2
Mobi (ISBN-13) 978-1-937584-97-9
Print (ISBN-13) 978-1-937584-95-5
1. Marijuana -- New York -- United States. 2. Drug traffic -- New York --
-- History. 3. True Crime/Organized Crime -- New York. I. Rogers, Toby.
II. Title

First Edition
10 9 8 7 6 5 4 3 2 1

Printed in the USA
Distribution to the Trade by:
Independent Publishers Group (IPG)
814 North Franklin Street
Chicago, Illinois 60610
312.337.0747
www.ipgbook.com

To the Busalacchi Clan

No Sympathy For The Devil: Toby Rogers, Journalism and The Mafia

By Jennifer Hershberger

The book you are about to read, should not have been written. At least not yet, that is.

Normally the true crime genre is about the past, when the subject at hand is either killed and sent to jail. The serial killer author waits until the serial killer is caught and there is a public trial and a conviction. The writer does not follow the serial killer around and watch him commit heinous acts of torture and murder.

Likewise, books about the Mafia are written after everybody has either been caught or killed.

Never before has a writer had such unprecedented access to an ongoing criminal organization. From the inside, Rogers exposes organized crime's world of secrecy, warped codes of honor and ancient laws of the street. He witnesses murder, high volume drug transactions, extortion, theft, prostitution and construction kickbacks.

Reflective of his other work, Toby Rogers doesn't just rely on subject interviews. He goes into the trenches, like his first book, *Ambushed*, where he infiltrated the Bush family just before George W. Bush began to put his 2000 presidential campaign together. During that investigation, Toby discovered that "W" was a cokehead in 1970's. The story broke on January 23, 2000 in the *Sunday Times* (London) and morphed into one of the iconic scandals of that presidential campaign.

Just as he did with the Bush family, Rogers experienced the New York City mobster highlife first hand, where celebrity and wealth overlap with drugs and the criminal underworld. It is a world of illusion, where no one suffers the consequences for their actions. A world where sociopaths are graciously rewarded for their inhumanity and indifference to cheating the system to get ahead.

As the marijuana legalization movement spreads across America, Toby Roger's *The Ganja Godfather* highlights the blood soaked reality that the argument against marijuana legalization bathes in. Those who stand against the regulated, tax paying, job creating, billion dollar marijuana economy emerging out west, inadvertently enable drug lords like the Ganja Godfather back east.

The Ganja Godfather serves as a metaphorical vortex through this historical tipping point, from the dark ages of the marijuana underground of the late twentieth century to the cannabis renaissance of the early twenty-first century.

The life of Silvio Eboli arches this history, which Rogers brilliantly captures in this book. Through skillful weaving of the personal and the historical, Rogers traces the life of this linear descendent of New York's original gangsters – Lucky Luciano, Vito Genovese and Silvio's grandparents, the Eboli brothers.

From the Dead Rabbits and the Five Points Gang to the mushroom Goddess cult of Bennington College – through prohibition, JFK, 9/11, Madoff and Occupy – *The Ganja Godfather* is truly breath taking in its scope.

But author Toby Rogers wrote much more than just another true crime tale, it is a microcosmic memoir of a generation that came of age between the end and the beginning of two millenniums.

With the innocent swag of Jack Kerouac and Hunter S. Thompson and the reflective insight of Michel Herr and Gary Smith, Toby Rogers' *The Ganja Godfather* is without a doubt Generation X's non-fiction high water mark. Like *On The Road* and *Fear and Loathing In Las Vegas*, it's mythos will endure in high school detention halls, rowdy college dorm rooms, and urban coffee houses across the globe for decades to come.

– Jennifer Hershberger is the author of *Single and Content*. She is from Cleveland, Ohio.

Eboli – Coat of Arms

Dinner With The Eboli Family: Costa Nostra, History and the Oral Tradition

We all have heard stories at the family dinner table. We hear them on holidays, at family barbecues and reunions. Stories that have been told and retold again and again. Fine-tuned or altered over the years and passed down from one to another for decades and generations. Stories about family members colliding with history – particularly if what they say doesn't jive with what's considered established or official history – are stories that tend to endure the longest.

How long did the family oral tradition keep alive Thomas Jefferson's affair with slave Sarah "Sally" Hemmings, whom Jefferson had six children with after his wife, Martha Wayles-Jefferson, died when the then future American president was only forty-four?

Exactly 163 years straddled Sarah Hemmings death in 1835 and 1998, when DNA testing finally showed that Jefferson did in fact have black offspring and living descendants with Hemmings.

A few years ago, I was interviewing relatives of Harriett Tubman in upstate New York. They told me that family elders said Tubman's back "looked like a maze," from whippings. It was a description I had never come across in the myriad of Tubman books published.

In my own family I was told my grandfather, Ralph Herrmann, soon after World War II ended in Europe – while serving in Germany – led a Dixieland band on Hitler's personal yacht for the Pentagon's core leadership overseas in Europe in May 1945. As the boat drifted down Germany's Rhine River, Generals Dwight D. Eisenhower, George S. Patton and Omar N. Bradley, threw a raucous, booze-soaked party with other top military brass and a horde of Nazi prostitutes to celebrate the end of the war in Europe.

Is it actually true? It is plausible. The U.S. and allied forces did in fact recover several of Hitler's yachts after WW II. Prostitution and alcohol consumption were rampant in the military overseas at the time. But all three of those generals, on Hitler's yacht together, drunk with prostitutes? It sounds like the story that may have been slightly embellished. It's hard to really prove or disprove.

Another family member of mine shared a dorm room at Boston University with Kelly Breslin, daughter of the iconic New York City journalist James "Jimmy" Breslin.

Breslin was one of the few journalists that witnessed the assassination of Malcolm X unfold at the Audubon Ballroom in Harlem, on February 21, 1965. He wrote about what he saw in the *New York Herald Tribune*, a time when papers ran several editions a day. In his first article, published under large banner headlines the morning after Malcolm's assassination, there was the sub-headline: "Police Rescue Two Suspects."

In the article Breslin reported that one suspect, Talmadge Hayer, was "taken to Bellevue Prison Ward and was sealed off by a dozen policemen. The other suspect was taken to Wadsworth Avenue Precinct, where the city's top policemen converged and began one of the heaviest investigations this city has ever seen."

Jimmy Berlin's front page sto on the assassination Malcolm for the *New York Herald Tribun* Between the *Tribune*'s mornir and evening editions, one su pect in New York Police custo vanished without explanation

The *New York Times* reported the same thing in their first morning edition after Malcolm's assassination. Their sub-headline read: "Police Hold Two For Questioning." According to the *Times*, New York Police Department Officer Thomas Hoy picked up a second suspect." As I brought him (suspect two) to the front of the ballroom, the crowd began beating me and the suspect," Officer Hoy told the *Times*.

The *Times* reported that Hoy "put this man – not otherwise identified for newsmen – into a police car to be taken to the Wadsworth Avenue station."

In the following editions published later that day, the *Times* and the *Tribune* – without any explanation – removed any mention of the second suspect from subsequent editions.

On the 40th anniversary of the Malcolm X assassination, February 21, 2005, I spoke to Jimmy Breslin about what he witnessed over the phone – I had gotten his number from Kelly. I called and was leaving a message when Breslin picked up. I told him who I was, and that I wanted to ask about what he witnessed in Harlem exactly forty years ago.

> Well I was supposed to receive a journalism award in Syracuse that evening, but I got tip (from the NYPD) that I should go up to Harlem to see Malcolm X speak. I sat way in the back smoking a Pall Mall cigarette.

When I asked Jimmy about the reports of a second suspect and his strange disappearance – both in his *Tribune* story and the *Times* piece – all of the sudden Breslin got quite cagey. He knew exactly what I was referring to and refused to talk any further.

> Fuck it, I don't want to know no more, that's it! I don't fucking know what is what. I don't know if there was two editions or one. I don't want to remember. I don't want to read it. Fuck it. Who cares! It's 2005, I … fucking dead and disinterested.

I couldn't believe my ears. Here was a journalist, a well-known journalist, who witnessed the assassination of a civil rights leader –

Jimmy Breslin, 40 years to the day of the assassination of Malcolm X February 21, 2005, confessed that the NYPD suggested he attend a speech by Malcolm X in Harlem. In that same interview Breslin has a meltdown when confronted about the disappearance of suspect two from his original story.

Aftermath of the assassination of Malcolm X, Audubon Ballroom, February, 21, 1965.

after receiving a tip from police. Two suspects are caught, and one disappears in police custody. And Breslin's response is I don't want to know no more?

I never did anything with the conversation I had with Breslin, until now, on the eve of the 50th anniversary of the Malcolm X Assassination. Yet I have told numerous family members about the incident since 2005, and I'm willing to bet the story might of slightly changed when others have retold it.

As I began to work on *The Ganja Godfather*, after conducting several interviews with the Eboli clan, I realized that they had a rich, extensive oral history that has lasted within the family long after Tommy and Patsy Eboli had gone. A history that at times, indeed felt like mythology. A history where nuances might just have been tweaked a little to add suspense to a late night family dinner conversation.

Nevertheless, I still felt compelled to document this remarkable American family. There is nothing that I wrote that is not rooted in the truth, but I cannot confirm for certain that every five o'clock shadow, every pin-stripped suit and fedora, and every Thomson- C-21 are. But the Eboli family's role in the rise of the Mafia in New York as well as the intricate part they played in the making of *The Godfather* in 1971 is unquestionably true and more than worthy of historical documentation.

Just as writers in the nineteenth century who covered Jesse James and Billy the Kid struggled to distinguish fact from myth along the outlaw trails of the "Wild West," so too is the history of Costa Nostra difficult to pin down in the twenty first century. That being said, it is still worth trying.

As for my own first hand experiences with the Eboli clan – because of the current, ongoing criminal activity some of them are involved in – many things had to be reworked in order to be able to publish this book. As Silvio joked, in order to "protect the guilty," dates, sequence, and whereabouts have been rearranged and slightly altered.

Writings from the 19th Century on Billy The Kid overlapped fact and sensationalized fiction in order to sell books.

But the essence of what I wrote is true.

The Ganja Godfather is no jailhouse memoir or some old dead man's tale. It is Costa Nostra, operating, now, on the streets of New York. Because of these unique and delicate circumstances, the challenge to get this story accurate and at the same protect my sources was daunting. After years of struggling with the narrative, I believe I have struck the right balance between presenting fact, yet still preserving the anonymity of "Silvio" Eboli; aka the Ganja Godfather.

– Toby Rogers, St. Paul Island, Alaska, 11/28/14

CHAPTER ONE

The Offer I Couldn't Refuse

Crime pays!
— Silvio Eboli

"Yo Kunta, break this up," Silvio said to me with a thick, New York Italian accent. He handed me a few nugs of Sour Diesel, turned around and continued to talk shop with a well known musician and producer from Brooklyn. His friend had cabbed over to Silvio's Lower East Side recording studio to grab a few "zips" before going out on tour.

It was early fall, 2009. It had been years since I last saw Silvio, but it was like a day had not gone by since we last spoke.

We grew up together and had been friends for over 25 years, yet tonight he asked me to meet to "talk business."

Silvio was playing a track, a song about Evel Knievel, from his latest recording session. The last line of the chorus of *Ride Evel Ride*, was "ride Evel ride, ride up to the sky."

"What sparked you to write about Evel ..." I had begun to ask before Silvio interrupted.

"Shut up," Silvio said while waving his arm at me in annoyance for interrupting the listening session.

Things had slightly changed since I last saw Silvio. The price and the quality of weed he sold had gone up. His customer base was more upscale and included a handful of well-known celebrities. Sour Diesel, flown in from California, went for $30 a gram, but the minimum order was three, two gram "tickets," totaling $180. His clients usually bought more than six grams per delivery, zips — or ounces — being the most popular weight of choice for the rich and famous.

Between 2001 and 2004, Silvio had bought pot in bulk from Native Americans in canoes on the St. Lawrence River between the New York and Canadian border. When that connection evaporated in 2005, he began FedExing pot from northern California to New York.

Silvio also now carried himself – clothes, body language and all – like a B-movie Mafia don.

"That's that best you can fucking do? I said break that shit up!"

After a fat spliff, we went back to the sound booth. Hanging on the back red brick wall was an Italian flag and a small portrait of Pope John Paul II – his official 1978 papal shot. In some Italian mob circles, images of Pope John Paul II are believed to offer good luck to their owner.

Silvio opened up a bass drum case filled with "tickets" along with dozens of zips and "QP's" (quarter pound) bagged and ready for sale. The intense high of the

Pope John Paul II, October 22, 1978.

Diesel was just as overwhelming as the smell of the bagged, green and purple plants.

"You hungry?" Silvio asked me, after his last sale of the evening.

"Starving."

We took a cab to the Grand Central Oyster Bar & Resturant. Silvio ordered two appetizers, a plate Oysters Rockefeller and a plate of Florida Stone Crabs, as well as a bottle of red wine and two shellfish platters, both with whole lobsters.

Silvio talked a lot about the past at the Oyster Bar that night, about growing up in Scarsdale together, and an upcoming high school anniversary he was on the fence about attending.

After we finished eating, he ordered even more food.

"Let's get down to brass tacks," Silvio said, after a couple shots of whiskey, a few beers and two more dozen raw oysters.

Silvio explained that Mark Jacobs from *New York Magazine* had approached him about a doing a feature on his life, only later to publish a long rambling exposition about weed in New York, briefly mentioning him as "Francis."

Disappointed with what was ultimately published, Silvio wanted to "reboot" the story and tell it his way.

This time, he wanted a writer he could totally trust.

"That's where you come in," Silvio told me.

I was taken aback.

Through the piles of empty seafood shells, I looked across the table. He was not just an old friend anymore. He was Silvio Eboli, grandson of some of New York's most notorious mobsters – the Genovese crime family, still carrying the torch of the "old ways" on the streets of New York  Vito Genovese

in an ongoing criminal drug operation. He was asking me to be his personal biographer.

The out of the blue phone call. The meeting with a music legend. The long and elaborate dinner.

Now it all made sense.

I stalled.

"I have to think about it. I don't want to wind up in a…"

"Tell you what," Silvio interrupted. He stood up, put on his leather overcoat and left me a white envelope on the table under the bill. "Think it over," Silvio said and left for his train.

When I got home, I counted the cash, a stack of hundred dollar bills. It was a ridiculous amount of money.

I met Silvio the next evening at S.P.Q.R., the priciest "ristorante" in Little Italy. This time he was surrounded by four gorgeous women, dates for the night. There was a Russian girl, a Swede, a Japanese girl and a Brazilian, elegantly dressed in evening gowns.

I looked at Silvio, and asked if its was "okay to…"

"None of these girls speak a word of English," Silvio informed me.

Through a phalanx of red wine bottles, lobster Alfredo and anti-pasta plates, I told him it was a go.

Little Italy, New York City.

"Where do you want to begin?" I asked.

"My family history would be a good start, don't you think?"

"That's an excellent segue Sil," I responded.

Silvio was shook. My tone telegraphed one thing. Envelopes of cash aside, I was not going to be his personal propaganda minister.

"I watched a bunch of Mafia and Genovese documentaries last night on YouTube, A&E, History Chanel, all the John Gotti ones too. None of them mention Tommy or Pasquale Eboli."

"Do you know why?" Silvo asked.

"No."

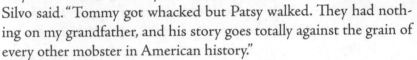

Tommy Eboli, 1952.

"Because Tommy and Patsy never got caught. There is no state propaganda lesson in their story, no Uncle Sam throwing them behind bars. Fuck, they ran circles around Uncle Sam and the FBI. The Feds knew they were Mafia, but they couldn't take them down," Silvo said. "Tommy got whacked but Patsy walked. They had nothing on my grandfather, and his story goes totally against the grain of every other mobster in American history."

"How so?" I asked.

"Patsy proved crime pays. And that's why he was stripped out of history. He doesn't fit the mold Uncle Sam wants for their mobsters. Patsy is the real deal, a mobster's mobster. And anyone in this business knows Patsy was the only motherfucker in U.S. Mafia history that won in the end."

"Patsy is the only one," Silvio reiterated one more time.

"What about you?" I joked.

Silvio ignored me and cut into his rare *"filetto alla griglia."*

As Silvio cut his steak, blood spilled on to his white, porcelain plate.

Parked outside, we all got in a limousine Silvio rented for the night. Inside the Russian girl opened a bottle of champagne. Glasses were filled and we toasted and drank. Silvio handed a pouch to the Brazilian girl. She rolled a blunt and lit up.

We pulled up to the rooftop nightclub, 230 Fifth and walked in. Silvio put his arms around the girls as they were guided to their cabana by a hostess, who he handed a hundred dollar bill after we were seated.

I looked around the over the top club and its views of Manhattan's skyline, and saw Rihanna walking by. Derek Jeter was there too, standing off to the side talking to a stunningly beautiful young woman.

A bottle of Gray Goose and Cristal soon arrived at the table. After a few shots, I began to think.

What the fuck have I gotten myself into?

While the music thumped and the girls all swirled around him, Silvio looked empty. The id inside Silvio had become insatiable since we last spoke years ago, and no amount of money, drugs or pussy was going to make him feel whole again. He had reached the mountain top and had it all and then some, but it was nothing more than a pile of quicksand, slowly devouring his soul in the process.

Silvio's eyes were cold and reptilian as he looked around Manhattan's elite inner circle. He was on top of the world, yet he was in total darkness and their was no way out.

Tommy Eboli

CHAPTER TWO

Cristo Si è Fermato a Eboli

There is no such thing as good money or bad money. There's just money.
– Charles "Lucky" Luciano

The Eboli family name derives from a small farming commune in Southern Italy, known for their olive oil and buffalo mozzarella cheese. The town of Eboli is also known for it's gripping poverty. The town's unofficial motto: *Cristo si è fermato a Eboli* ('Christ stopped at Eboli'), which also is the title of the book by anti-fascist artist/writer Dr. Carlo Levi about life in Eboli through forced exile after Benito Mussolini took over Italy.

Levi explained the meaning:

First English edition of Levi's memoir.

> The title of the book comes from an expression, "Christ stopped short of here, at Eboli," which means, in effect, that they feel they have been bypassed by Christianity, by morality, by history itself – that they have somehow been excluded from the full human experience.

Tommaso Eboli was born June 13, 1911 in Scisciano (in the province of Naples), Italy. He was born to Louis Eboli and Madalena Maddalone. Madalena died when Tommaso was young and in the old Italian tradition, Madalena's younger sister Gianna took over as Tommy's mother. Louis married Gianna and moved his family to New York City.

On August 10, 1924, Tommaso's younger brother Pasquale Eboli was born in Queens, NY.

Together, despite the age gap – the two Eboli brothers ran through the streets of New York City, and quickly got tenderized in its ways. By the time the Eboli brothers grew into adulthood, "Costa

Nostra" had already been well established in New York and branched well beyond the city limits.

The American Mafia grew out the New York City gang culture of the mid-19th Century, when the Irish-Catholic Dead Rabbits and Plug Uglies roamed the streets of the Lower East Side and the "Five Points" of Paradise Square. For decades they battled for turf with the "Bowery Boys," Protestant American-born "Natives," who were born in America, and who's kin fought and died in the American Revolution.

July 4-5 1857: Catholic Dead Rabbits and Protestant Bowery Boys fought in a city wide gang war.

The immigrants of downtown Manhattan were terrorized by the Bowery Boys and their own gang culture paralleled the abuse they were subjected to. Immigrants like the legendary Dead Rabbit, "Hell Cat Maggie" ambushed the Bowery Boys in alleyways and saloons with her razor-sharp brass fingernails, avenging "Native" oppression in her community. Throughout the 1840s and '50s immigrants gangs valiantly fought off the native gangs in the streets, that at times shut down several city blocks for days.

When the Civil War came to a close in 1865, Manhattan was still recovering from the vicious draft riots from 1863 that virtually destroyed much of the city. Yet, immigrants still poured into Manhattan from

1863 New York City Draft Riots.

all over and the gang culture on the streets reflected the diversity of nationalities that populated downtown .

Jewish gangs, like the "Yiddish Black Hand" and the "Coin Collectors" and the infamous Italian/Sicilian Five Points Gang emerged on the scene in New York.

Five Points intersection, George Catlin -1827

They too – like everyone else in the city – had to claw and scratch in the streets to make any headway for their people.

The Five Points Gang got its name from "Paradise Square" where five streets in the city met: Mulberry, Anthony (now Worth), Cross (now Park), Orange (now Baxter), and Water (extinct). Five Points was founded by Sicilian, Paolo Antonio Vaccarelli, who went by "Paul Kelly." Kelly was also a professional boxer and used his fight earnings to start up brothels and clubs all around the city.

Kelly, who was fluent in English, Italian, Spanish and French, hired Johnny Torrio to be his second in command. Kelly later recruited Alphonse Gabriel "Al" Capone and Salvatore Lucania, aka Charles "Lucky" Luciano into Five Points and worked closely with Meyer Suchowljansky, aka "Meyer Lansky" and Benjamin "Bugsy" Siegel.

"Paul Kelly"

Johnny Torrio

Al Capone

Lucky Luciano

Meyer Lansky

Bugsy Siegel

Through Kelly and these five New York City streets kids, the modern American Mafia was born.

Luciano, born on November 24, 1897 in Lercara Friddi, Sicily, moved with his family to Manhattan's Lower East Side when he was ten.

Luciano sold hats on the streets of New York for $7 a week, until one day he

Luciano in Italy.

quit to become a full time street hustler after winning $244 with dice. It is rumored that Luciano got his nickname "Lucky" after he was subjected to a serious beat down in his youth by much older adults that should have killed him.

In October, 1929, he took another beating, this time his throat was slashed and he was left for dead in Staten Island. Luciano became a neighborhood legend on the Lower East Side, when the local papers drummed up the story, particularly the fact that Luciano refused to report his attackers to authorities. Luciano later told the Eboli brothers in 1953 that it was the New York Police Department, who almost beat him to death.

Luciano recruited Vito Genovese and Frank Costello into Five Points and together they moved into bootlegging liquor.

During prohibition, the U.S. Government inadvertently created vast sums of wealth for criminal organizations that were able to import liquor – mainly from Scotland, Canada or the Caribbean – into America. By 1925, Luciano, at age 28, was raking in $12 million a year, some of which went to bribing law enforcement and politicians in New York.

Tommaso Ebloi idolized Luciano and Kelly, and as teenager began bootlegging booze for Luciano in the early 1920's. Tommy followed in Kelly's footsteps and became a prizefighter in the early 1930's. He called himself "Tommy Ryan," after a popular neighborhood fighter who had retired.

Luciano and Genovese met Tommy after a fight, and he was immediately hired as Genovese's bodyguard and hit-man. Luciano

Frank Costello

Vito Genovese

was under boss for Giuseppe "Joe The Boss" Masseria, who in the 1920's was the Mafia kingpin of New York.

Joe "The Boss" Masseria

Meanwhile, Sicilian boss Don Vito Ferro, who controlled the Sicilian city of Castellammare del Golfo, wanted to take over New York and its bootlegging operations. He brought in Salvatore Maranzano to muscle everyone else out. Maranzano hired Joseph "Joe Bananas" Bonanno, Stefano "The Undertaker" Magaddino, Joseph Profaci, and Joe Aiello to wipe out Masseria and his crew.

Masseria had Luciano, Genovese , Albert "Mad Hatter" Anastasia, Alfred Mineo, Willie Moretti, Joe Adonis, Frank Costello and Tommy Eboli in his crew.

What started out with a few liquor truck robberies, escalated fast into a total mob bloodbath. It was a turf war of epic proportions.

It was also a generational war. Maranazo and his crew were called the "Moustache Petes" for their backwards, rural Sicilian ways and long, old fashioned mustaches. Masseria, Genovese and Tommy were dubbed the "Young Turks" for wearing pin striped suits, fedora hats and a willingness to work with nationalities besides their own.

Killings popped off back and forth until Luciano came up with plan to end the war. He sided with Maranazo and agreed to whack Masseria in turn for becoming Maranazo's underboss.

On April 15, 1931, Luciano had dinner with Masseria at Nuova Villa Tammaro, a Brooklyn restaurant at Coney Island. Sitting a few tables away was Anastasia, Genovese, Tommy Eboli, Joe Adonis, and Siegel. When Luciano went to use the restroom, his hit squad opened fire on Masseria. Tables tipped, silverware clinked as people running in terror poured out of the restaurant front door.

April 15, 1931: Masseria whacked by Tommy Eboli in Coney Island, New York

Witnesses said that Tommy, wearing a pinstriped suit, fedora, and five o'clock shadow opened fire on Masseria with a Thompson-21 – a 45-caliber sub machine gun – that he pulled out of a violin case. As he fired Tommy puffed on a fat cigar to mask his face. He sprayed whole joint with bullets leaving the walls and the ceiling riddled with holes.

The "Tommy Gun."

A few years back, Capone had bought a truck load of Thompson-21s – with the round "Type C" drum magazine – at wholesale and sold them to everyone he could. It was known on the street as the "Tommy Gun" and later the "Chicago Typewriter," and eventually all of Hollywood's gangsters and criminals used the gun in films.

Ciro "The Artichoke King" Terranova was waiting for everyone outside in the getaway car, but when he heard all of Tommy's shots, he started to tremble with fear. As everyone piled in, the Artichoke King choked, and Siegel had to push him over and drive off.

The *New York Times* reported that "the police have been unable to learn definitely [what happened]."

"The Artichoke King."

With Masseria out of the way, Maranzano took over the city. Maranzao split up the New York Costra Nostra into five "families." He declared himself – *capo di tutti capi* or "boss of all bosses" and ran the families in the traditional power structure that originated on the lemon farms of Sicily in the mid-19th Century.

Maranzano was victorious in New York, but his reign as Boss was short lived. Luciano was still plotting to rub out Maranzano as Maranzano was looking to do the same to Luciano.

On September 10, 1931, Maranzano requested that Luciano meet him at his Park Avenue office. Luciano brought along his "Jew Crew" of Sigiel, Samuel "Red" Levine and Bo Weinberg. They showed up early and caught Maranzano off guard.

After they stabbed Maranzano, Luciano took the throne of "Mafia King" of New York. He quickly ordered hits on every "Moustache Pete" in the city. Tommy Eboli was right in the middle of it all as the streets filled with Sicilian blood.

The newspapers dubbed it "The Night of Sicilian Vespers."

Luciano went on to become the most powerful crime boss in Mafia history. He moved in the feared Vito Genovese as his underboss, which automatically moved Tommy up the ranks too.

Now that he was in charge, Luciano wanted to restructure and modernize the mob and try to avoid such hostiles in the future.

He set up the "Commission" which consisted of the boss of each of the Five Families. There they openly discussed problems between each other and charted their future together, at least so they thought. Luciano still pulled all the strings of course, but he let the Commission have sway over minor issues.

For instance, Luciano wanted to do away with the traditional Sicilian ceremony *"amico nostro," or* becoming a "made-man." The commission and Lansky asked Luciano to allow the practice to continue so young people had rituals that promoted family obedience.

Luciano also had the Commission hear proposals and grievances of criminal gangs from other ethnicities.

One issue that went before the Commission in 1935 was a request from Arthur Flegenheimer, aka "Dutch Schultz" to assassinate New York Governor Herbert H. Lehman's newly appointed U.S. Special Prosecutor Thomas E. Dewey, who was investigating the New York Mafia and circling around Schultz.

Luciano and the Commission unanimously agreed that killing Dewey was an extremely bad idea that would provoke a massive law enforcement crackdown that could get them all locked up. Schultz dug in and demanded another meeting to "clarify" Luciano's position. Schultz even

"Dutch" Schultz

went so far as to convert to Catholicism from Judaism to try and persuade Luciano to change his mind.

When Luciano and the Commission refused Schultz's second request to whack Dewey, Schultz said he was going to do it anyway.

Luciano and the Commission quickly decided to whack Schultz and had Tommy Eboli kill him on October 24, 1935, in a Newark, New Jersey bar. After the hit, Luciano discovered that Schultz had ordered a custom built, airtight, waterproof safe, where he stashed $7 million in cash and bonds

October 24, 1935: "Dutch" Schultz whacked by Tommy Eboli in Newark, NJ.

in and had it hid somewhere up in the Catskills. Luciano, Genovese and the Eboli brothers spent a considerable amount of time upstate looking for Schultz's loot but all of them came up short.

People still gather annually in the Catskills to search for the "lost treasure of Dutch Schultz."

When Dewey heard about went down, he thanked Luciano by issuing an arrest warrant for him and shutting down two hundred of Lucky's brothels. Luciano got a tip about the warrant even before the ink was dry and took off to Hot Spring, Arkansas, where he was subsequently captured. After Arkansas Attorney General Carl E. Bailey refused a $50,000 cash bribe, Luciano was extradited back to New York to face sixty counts of compulsory prostitution in April of 1936.

Thomas E. Dewey: In 1948, Dewey lost the presidential race to Harry S. Truman.

Luciano was sentenced to thirty to fifty years and sent to Sing Sing Correctional Facility in Ossining, New York. He was later moved to Clinton Correctional Facility in Dannemora, New York, where he was allowed to have a personal chef cook for him three times a day in a private kitchen. He also used his power to get the materials inside to build a small Catholic church on the prison yard – the only free standing church within the entire New York State correctional system – with two original doors built into the altar that came from Portuguese explorer Ferdinand Magellan's *Victoria*, the first ship to successfully circumnavigate the world.

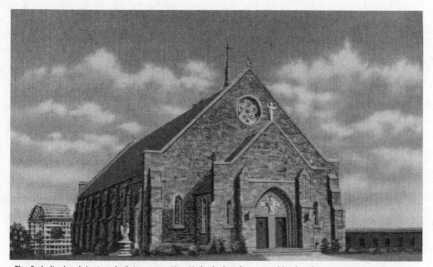

The Catholic church Luciano built in upstate New York- declared a national landmark in 1991. Her benefactor was one of New York State's best kept secrets- until now.

It is known as the *Church of St. Dismas, the Good Thief* and was placed on the list of National Register of Historic Places in 1991. The church – built between 1939 and 1941 – has been estimated to have cost $250,000 to build at that time. While celebrated as an iconic piece architecture in upstate New York, hardly anyone knows the real history of how it was built and who exactly paid for her construction. According to the towns official history the money was "raised from private sources," including a $25,000 organ, a "donation" from two unnamed "Jewish benefactors," who were Lansky and Sigel. The Eboli brothers also chipped in some cash for the project.

Luciano made Genovese acting boss, while he was still appealing his case. When the United States Supreme Court refused to hear Luciano's final appeal in 1938, he made Frank Costello the Boss after Genovese fled to Italy with $750,00 in cash to avoid murder charges in 1937.

Luciano pushed every way he could to get out of prison, but Uncle Sam was not interested.

In 1942, Luciano's luck changed. After the attacks Pearl Harbor in December of 1941, the U.S Navy needed accurate intelligence regarding New York's waterfronts. The U.S. Navy contacted Lansky to arrange a deal with Luciano.

The U.S Justice Department was willing to commute Luciano's sentence if he promised the U.S. Navy all the available intelligence he had on the waterfronts and prevented dockworker strikes during the war.

Vito Genovese worked with Uncle Sam in 1943 when the allies invaded Italy. He became an U.S. Army "interpreter/liaison officer" at the U.S. Army headquarters in Naples, where a year later he was arrested for stealing army trucks, flour and sugar from the base. Genovese was brought back to America to face the outstanding murder charges, but all of the prosecution's witnesses were suddenly killed off. One witness, Peter LaTempa, was in protective services – requested by the Brooklyn District Attorney's office – when he died after taking his gallstone medication in a guarded cell at the Raymond Street Jail. It was later discovered that LaTempa had enough poison in his blood stream to "kill eight horses."

After the charges were dropped, the judge in the case said from the bench to Genovese before releasing him.

> By devious means, among which were the terrorizing of witnesses, kidnapping them, yes, even murdering those who give evidence against you, you have thwarted justice time and again. I cannot speak for the jury, but I believe that if there were even a shred of corroborating evidence, you would have been condemned to the (electric) chair.

On January 3, 1946, then Governor Thomas E. Dewey commuted Luciano's sentence on the condition that he would be deported to Italy. Luciano, never obtaining U.S. citizenship, reluctantly agreed to the deal.

On February 9, 1947 – his last night in America – Luciano had pasta dinner on a freighter with a few associates that included the Eboli brothers. Luciano arranged that Tommy and Patsy would smuggle cash into Sicily for Luciano, where he would eventually be hiding out.

The next day Luciano boarded a ship in Brooklyn and set off for Naples. Other than a cargo of flour, he was the only passenger on board.

Tommy and Pasquale, who went by "Patsy Ryan," flew to Sicily several times a year with suitcases of cash for Luciano. Over time Luciano grew fond of Patsy, and treated him like son. Luciano despised Tommy and only tolerated him for Patsy's sake.

Patsy fell in love with Sicily and would immerse himself in the old ways and traditions that were disappearing in Italy and he was unable experience in America.

During World War II, Tommy retired from professional fighting and moved into training and management. He had several fighters under his wing, including middleweight Rocky Castellani and light-heavyweight Vincent Louis Gigante.

After prohibition ended, fight fixing became a big racket for the mob. Tommy and Patsy were quite good at turning fighters into tank artists, to a take dive for a larger cut under-the-table.

"Nothing is better than fixed fight," Patsy told family, "it just rains money."

First Patsy used his natural charm and his power of persuasion on a fighter. If that didn't work, Tommy and his crew would persuade fighters by other means.

Tommy Eboli exiting court, 1960s.

Tommy had a reputation in the mob and the boxing world as a hot head. "He would walk into a bar and if somebody looked at him the wrong way, you might never see that person again," an elderly mob insider said.

"That was the way of Tommy Eboli, always yelling, swinging, threatening – in clubs, alleyways, wherever. People were terrified when he walked in. He had no honor, respect or decency in him. Besides Patsy and a few family members, everybody hated him in New York," the elderly mobster added.

Tommy's temper was on full display at Madison Square Garden on January 11, 1952. Tommy and boxing promoter Al Weill had fixed a fight between Rocky Castellani and Erine "The Rock" Durando. It was agreed by both men and Durando that Castellani, Tommy's fighter, would be declared victor.

But something went amiss in the sixth round when Durando knocked down Castellani. In the next round Durando knocked Castellani down again and the referee Ray Miller quickly called a TKO victory for Durano.

Tommy stood up in his fighters corner, dismayed at what just unfolded. He looked around the Garden, his mind went into slow motion as popcorn and peanuts flew by his peripheral vision. As he realized that he had been double crossed, Tommy looked out into the first few rows of seats, looked at family, friends and associates – all burned along with him. He turned to Patsy in the front row. Patsy didn't have to say a word, just a nod is all it took.

Wearing a corner lab coat, Tommy slipped between the ropes walked over to Miller – a former boxer himself – who gave Tommy a fuck you grin. Tommy wiped it off with a vicious left hook and right hand lead. Miller hit the canvass with loud thud as others pulled Tommy into his corner. The crowd roared with primal rage at Tommy's reckless response to Miller's shady TKO

January 11, 1952: Tommy Eboli KO's referee Ray Miller in Madison Square Garden, New York City and is banned from boxing for life.

call. They knew they would never see Tommy in a ring again and gave him a standing ovation on the way out of the ring, showering him in popcorn, peanuts and beer on the way to locker room.

The promoter Weill walked in and Tommy didn't hesitate for a moment before kicking him to the ground, and stomping on him some more.

"We had a fucking deal, you scum rat!" Tommy yelled as he pummeled Weill.

Two weeks later Tommy was indicted on two counts of assault. He plead guilty in the Spring and was sentenced to sixty days in prison on reduced charges.

The New York Athletic Commission banned Tommy from boxing for life. Up until Mike Tyson chewed off Evander Holyfield's ear in 1997, Tommy's outburst in 1952 was considered one of the most sickening moments in boxing history.

When Tommy was released, Patsy drove his older brother to midtown for drinks at the Plaza Hotel's Oak Room, not one of their usual hang out spots. He was trying to make a point to his older brother.

"Now that your through with boxing, we got to think outside our lots. We either got to move up or go sideways," Patsy told Tommy.

"Why don't we do both?" Tommy asked.

Tommy let his brother invest his money into legitimate business ventures. Within a few years Tommy and Patsy

The Brothers Eboli, following booking at Elizabeth St. Precinct, brothers Eboli, Patsy, left, and Tommy, right leave in company of detectives (center). Thomas Eboli (nee Tommy Ryan), manager of Rocky Castellani, was charged with assaulting referee Ray Mille.(Photo By: Arthur Buckley/NY Daily News via Getty Images)

owed several successful distribution companies, such as jukebox supplier Jet Music Corporation, and Tryan Cigarette Vending Service, Inc. They also owed several nightclubs – including a few gay bars – and invested heavily in the music industry. Tommy also controlled several Hudson River docks under the table.

Tommy also killed for Genovese regularly. After a hit, Tommy and Patsy would drive up New York Route West 17(now known as "old Route 17) highway and get off at Swan Lake. There they would dump the bodies in the water tied to gym weights. Patsy like dumping bodies in Swan Lake because the lake was right off the exit and was far enough outside their orbit without driving far.

In late 1956, Tommy and Patsy flew to Sicily to drop off a suitcase of cash for Luciano. After getting caught in Havana, Luciano had given up trying to get back into the United States, and accepted his fate that he would never return America.

Luciano was against the Genovese crime family getting involved with drug trafficking.

Tommy also brought Luciano a verbal request from Genovese. He wanted to whack Costello and take over as Boss.

Luciano shut it down. He knew why Genovese and Tommy wanted to kill Costello. It was drugs. Lucia-

29

no and Costello did not want the mob involved in selling narcotics, Genovese and Tommy did.

When Tommy and Patsy got to New York, they told Genovese the bad news.

"This whole drug business, its bigger than Lucky, its bigger than all of us and if we don't get involved someone else will," Patsy said to Genovese.

Genovese decided to go ahead and whack Costello anyway, and asked Tommy to set it up. For the first and only time, Tommy chose to find someone else to do the job. He asked his old fighter Gigante, who stupidly agreed to do the kill.

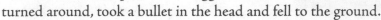

On May 2, 1957, Tommy drove Gigante in a black Cadillac to the lobby of the Majestic at 115 Central Park West and the corner of 72nd Street, where Costello had an apartment. Gigante waited in the lobby until Costello arrived and walked towards the elevator.

Gigante pulled out his .38-caliber handgun and pointed it at Costello's head.

"This is for you Frank!" Gigante yelled at Costello before he pulled the trigger. Costello

Vincent Louis "Chin" Gigante

turned around, took a bullet in the head and fell to the ground.

Gigante took off, jumped into Tommy's getaway car and they sped off.

"You got him?" Tommy asked.

"Yeah, its done" Gigante responded, "right in the fucking head."

But Costello survived the hit. The bullet only grazed him after Gigante gave him a "heads up" before firing only one shot.

Costello may have survived the hit, but he was rattled enough to agree to resign.

On November 14, 1957, Costello and Genovese held a summit at the home of mobster Joseph "Joe the Barber" Barbara in Apalachin, New York, a small upstate hamlet. Over a hundred mobsters from all over the United States, Canada and Italy showed up to this unique, one of a kind gathering.

"Joe the Barber"

At the meeting, which also included Tommy and Patsy, Costello announced his retirement and his successor to those in attendance.

The Cosa Nostra men (l. to r.) Attorney Jack Wasserman, Carlos Marcello, Santo Trafficante, Frank Ragano, Attorney Anthony Carollo, Frank Cagliano and John Marcello at La Stella Restaurant.

Genovese stood up and hugged Costello and accepted his new role as Boss.

Genovese declared that Tommy would be his underboss.

Outside the meeting, local law enforcement noticed the dozens of expensive cars with out of state plates parked all over the side streets. After setting up road blocks, the cops raided the meeting, making over 60 arrests.

Many, including Tommy and Patsy, escaped on foot in the woods.

But the busts had an even bigger impact, in the press and within the federal government. It proved beyond a shadow of a doubt, that the Mafia had mushroomed into a gigantic national and international crime syndicate.

Genovese quickly moved the mob into the illegal drug trade, but was tripped up by the Commission. Orchestrated by Luciano, the Commission set Genovese up in 1958 – less than a year after taking over as Boss – and he was arrested on drug trafficking charges.

In 1959, Genovese was sentenced to 15 years at Atlanta Federal Penitentiary in Atlanta, Georgia.

Genovese chose Tommy to become acting Boss.

Less than three years later, on January, 26 1962, Salvatore Lucania died at age 64 in Naples, Italy.

CHAPTER THREE

Blood Cries For Blood

Justice is a game.
— Bob Dylan

Tommy's first few years as acting Boss of the Genovese family went rather smoothly, minus Washington's public inquiry into the Mafia and the assassination of President John F. Kennedy. Tommy told family that Oswald was not the only shooter that awful day in Dallas, Texas on November 22 ,1963. According to what Tommy knew while "Oswald was shooting at Kennedy, a secret serviceman in the car behind pulled out a large shotgun and blew the presidents brains out."

It was something that he believed got buried by the Warren Commission. As out of left field it may appear, there are some interesting statements by witnesses on the record that support what Tommy told family.

Texas Senator Ralph Yarborough was seated directly behind the follow up car to the president in the motorcade. He told a reporter from the *Chicago Sun Times* published on November 23, 1963.

> I saw a secret serviceman seated in the car ahead of us reach down and pull out an automatic weapon or rifle. I smelled gun powder. It clung to the car nearly all the way to the hospital.

Yarborough appears to omit one glaring detail in this statement. He does not confirm or deny the smell of gunpowder came from the weapon of the secret serviceman. Yarborough could have said the gunpowder did not come from the a weap-

On the morning of November 22, 1963, President John F. Kennedy delivered a speech to thousands of Texans in downtown Fort Worth.

on fired from the secret service follow up car, if that was the case. But he leaves it open for reader to interpret themselves.

In subsequent interviews decades later Yarborough elaborated on what he witnessed on November 22, 1963 in the *Dallas Times Herald* on March 28, 1975 and the *Paris Texas News* on November 13, 1983. In both interviews, he sets up the same odd omission.

> I have hunted all my life and handled all kinds of weapons in the army. I knew they were rife shots and there were three of them. No more. A second or two later I smelled gunpowder. I always found that strange. Because being familiar with firearms – I could never see how you could smell the gunpowder if it came from the rifle in that high building. You don't smell gun powder unless your up wind of it and it blows in your face.

Yarborough was not the only one in the motorcade route who smelled gun powder or saw a secret serviceman pointing an automatic weapon at the president's car. Dallas Mayor Earl Cabell's wife Elizabeth Cabell – who was also in the presidential motorcade – told the Warren Commission "investigating" the Kennedy assassination.

Earl and Elizabeth Cabell.

> Well I turned to Earl to say 'Earl that was a shot.' And just as soon as I got the words out two second shots rang out. I was acutely aware of the smell of gunpowder.

Mayor Cabell told the Warren Commission:

> I heard the shots. There a long pause between the first and the second shot than between second and third shots. We could tell there was a lot of confusion in the presidents car – a lot of activity. A secret service man ran to that car. From out of nowhere one secret serviceman waved a sub-machine gun.

Dallas Patrolman Earl Brown, who was on the overpass over Elm, told the Warren Commission.

> We saw the car coming with the president and as it passed underneath. I look down and see this officer. He had this gun and

he was swinging it all around. It looked like a machine gun. And the president was all sprawled down.

Secret Serviceman Winston Lawson, who was in the front car of the presidential motorcade, mentions the agent's name in a singed statement on December 1, 1963.

I noticed agent (George)Hickey stand up in the follow up car with an automatic weapon. I first thought he fired at someone.

Secret Serviceman George Hickey wrote a singed statement himself on November 30, 1963 that totally contradicts what every other witness saw go down in Dallas on November 22, 1963.

At the end of the third shot, I reached down to the bottom of the car and picked up the AR-15 rifle – cocked and loaded it – and sat part way up the car and looked about. At this point we passed under the overpass and as a result left the scene of the shooting.

It is a very telling statement. First Hickey states he reached for the AR-15 "at the end of the third shot," and then he "cocked and loaded it."

According to secret servicemen Roy Kellerman, who was in charge of the Secret Service that day of the assassination and sat in the front seat of the president's car, told the Warren Commission.

We have a AR-15. It's out of it's case. It won't be shown. It could be lying on the floor(of the car) but she is "ready to go."

"Ready to go" in law enforcement circles means a weapon is *already* cocked and loaded and a bullet is in the chamber. All that is left to do is lift the safety, aim and shoot.

Sam Hallimond who stood on the overpass, told the Sheriff's Department in Dallas in a voluntary statement on the day of the Kennedy Assassination.

After the first shot, a Secret Serviceman, raised up with a machine gun and dropped back down in his seat.

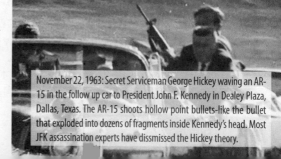

November 22, 1963: Secret Serviceman George Hickey waving an AR-15 in the follow up car to President John F. Kennedy in Dealey Plaza, Dallas, Texas. The AR-15 shoots hollow point bullets-like the bullet that exploded into dozens of fragments inside Kennedy's head. Most JFK assassination experts have dissmissed the Hickey theory.

Jean Hill stood on the side of the road less then 20 feet from Kennedy and told the Sheriff's Department in Dallas on the day of the Kennedy assassination in a voluntary statement.

> I saw the president grab his chest and fall forward. Then I think
> I saw a few plain clothes(officers) shooting back.

When Hill testified to the Warren Commission about return fire from the secret service, Arlen Spector – who conducted the interview with her – instead of following up with the witness about her seeing others "firing" a weapon in Dealey Plaza during the assassination, he quickly changed the subject to something else entirely.

Yarborough was never called to testify at the Warren Commission. Nor were several other witnesses who were interviewed by the Dallas Police the day of the assassination.

The Warren Commission also never explained how one bullet ricocheted through Kennedy and Texas Governor John Connolly and was later found intact, while a hollow point bullet that hit Kennedy in the head exploded on impact inside the president's skull. Dr. James Humes – who conducted the autopsy on Kennedy at Bethesda Naval Hospital – described seeing "30 to 40" bullet fragments inside the Kennedy's brain. That ballistic information alone proves that two guns were used to assassinate President Kennedy.

The intact bullet- an Austrian Mannlicher 6.5x52 mm roun that reportedly went through both Kennedy and Texas Govern John Connally and found on a stretcher at Parkland Memor Hospital. The Carcano bolt action rifle- Model 91/38- found the sixth floor of the Texas School Depository could not have fir the hollow point bullet that killed Kennedy.

Tommy also said the Mob and the CIA coordinated whacking Oswald. Which, if true, could explain why it was so peaceful between the Mafia and the U.S. Government after the assassination.

Five years later, when Robert F. Kennedy was gunned down in Los Angeles on June 5, 1968, Tommy got loaded and was overheard saying "lone gunman my ass, security was in on it, they always are."

If there had been a "peace" between the Mob and Uncle Sam, it was broken on September 22, 1966, when Tommy was busted in the

VIP room at the La Stella restaurant in Queens, along with Carlo Gambino, Carlos Marcello, Santo Trafficante, Joe Colombo, Aniello Dellacroce, and Mike Miranda.

Tommy was subpoenaed several times to testify in court in the mid and late 60s, but he would leak to the *New York Times* that he had a heart attack to avoid testifying.

Santo Trafficante being released after bust at La Stella Restaurant, Sept. 22, 1966.

Vito Genovese

On February 14, 1969, Genovese died in prison. The tabloid press printed that after Genovese's funeral Patsy and Genovese's wife, Anna Genovese, had begun having an affair after Vito was sent to prison. They ran pictures of Patsy and Anna Genovese at each others side at Vito's funeral.

Tommy became Boss directly after Genovese was buried, and Patsy was the first one to kiss his ring.

Tommy's reign as crime boss was erratic as his personality. At Commission meetings, he would show up late loaded on drugs. He would "ramble on and on" making "absolutely no sense whatsoever" one mobster said

The Commission began to hold meetings without Tommy being present, or even aware they were taking place.

"Tommy was a mess with drugs, and he was not well liked. It was obvious to everyone involved that his time as Boss would be short lived," the mobster said.

Nurse wheels Thomas Eboli aka Tommy Ryan from hearing room after he collapsed on witness stand.(Photo By: George Mattson/NY Daily News via Getty Images)

Tommy asked the Commission for a $4 million loan to set up the Eboli clan in the drug business. Within the first week of operation police made a raid and seized all the cash and the heroin. Without the means to pay the Commission back, it put Tommy in even more hot water. The Eboli clan believed it was all a set up, and the cops gave the money back to the Commission, minus their take.

Still, this did not stop Tommy from doing whatever the fuck he wanted. Tommy used his power as Boss to settle old scores and exact revenge on those he felt slighted by.

Tommy enjoyed killing, especially people that he believed truly deserved it.

> "Tommy was a little out of his mind, but he was a emotional guy. He loved his family and children, and he had a strong code of ethics. Tommy hated men who preyed on children. That was on the top of his list of traits in people he hated.

For years Tommy had begged Genovese to let him to whack Salvatore "Sally Burns" Granello for raping children. Genovese refused. Granello was a good friend of Genovese and was a "top earner for the family."

Throughout the 1960s, Granello had "taken advantage of several young girls," and "is known to be extremely rough with his female companions" according to Granello's FBI files.

One of the girls, a 14-year-old who lived on the Lower East Side Granello allegedly impregnated. The girl had a son, and informants for the FBI said the child "resembles GRANELLO to a great extent." The FBI learned that Granello was "barred from the neighborhood due to the ill feeling which resulted from the affair," and "this restriction is being enforced by several underworld figures due to the attitude of the local population." Yet Granello, an informant told agents raped another "young girl" on the Lower East Side in 1961.

Granello raped many more children in Greenwood Lake, NY where he would spend his summers at a lakefront bungalow he owned. An informant told the FBI that Granello "had sexually assaulted a 15 year old girl at Greenwood Lake, sometime between May and August, 1959," and "the subject is supposed to have paid the girl's father $15,000.00 in order to compromise the alleged rape."

In June on 1963, a family of another child who was raped by Granello filed a criminal complaint against Granello but the local judge threw the case out weeks later for "lack of corroboration"

A June 13, 1963 FBI memorandum reads:

Subject [Granello] acquainted with [girl] approximately five years and latter is an associate of subject's children.

[Girl] suffers from nerve injury in her back and currently under medical treatment. Granello has discussed with [girl] and her parents the possibility of consulting a NYC specialist re her physical condition. He has also discussed the possibility of having her employed as a model.

On June 10 last, Granello called [girl] and requested her to meet him at his summer residence. He stated he wished to discuss tentative appointments with the specialist and a model agency. [Girl] allegedly appeared at the subject's residence in her bathing suit at a time when the subject was alone. She posed in the bathing suit and in the nude for pictures taken by Granello with [girl's] camera. Granello removed the film and maintained possession of the same. Thereafter, Granello allegedly had intercourse with her. [Girl] advised investigating officers that she was too frightened to protest at the time, but later advised her boyfriend, [name redacted] of the occurrence.

Granello told [girl] that he would take her to consult the specialist in NYC on June 11 last. However, in the event his chauffeur was unable to pick her up he gave her $20 for bus fare to NYC.

Following disclosure of the alleged rape by [girl] to [her boyfriend] the latter suggested that she advise her parents and thereafter, [girl's] mother advised the NYS police. [Girl] was examined on the evening of June 11 by Doctor [name redacted] Greenwood Lake, New York, who acknowledged that [girl] had sexual relations but was unable to determine the time or previous chastity of [girl] due to the lapse of time since the occurrence.

On July 26, 1963, the *New York Daily News* published a story quoting Granello response to the dismissals of his statutory rape charges – *"I'm glad to have been vindicated of this terrible thing. Justice has prevailed."*

When Tommy took over as Boss in 1969, he held a meeting with Granello. Tommy told him that his days of raping children were over.

A Columbo mobster who was at the meeting told a FBI informant what went down between Tommy and Granello. The FBI flies state:

> [Informant] stated as the discussion went on, it grew into a violent stage and GRANELLO made statements to EBOLI that he had been responsible for all of his son's troubles and that it was not inconceivable that he, GRANELLO, could cause trouble to EBOLI and a lot of his friends for their broken promises. According to [informant] EBOLI supposedly told GRANELLO to stop and think and watch what he was saying. GRANELLO supposedly made remarks to the effect "you can't shut me up and what I say can even go as high as you." When GRANELLO left, the informant's sources understand EBOLI gave out a "hit" contract on GRANELLO

According to the FBI, the 5'6, 250 pound Granello was last seen on the night of September 24, 1970, slurping clams at Vincent's Clam Bar. As Granello exited the restaurant, Tommy and his goons grabbed him and threw him in a van.

The FBI said "the murder took place in a coffee shop on Elizabeth Street between Houston and Prince Streets, NYC."

Vincent's Clam Bar, New York City

Tommy and his muscle brought Granello downstairs to the coffee shop basement and worked him over. Tommy wrapped his hands and did "three rounds" on Granello, punching him over and over while being held up. When there was nothing left to break and no more teeth to smash, Tommy was out of breath.

Granello's face was a crimson mask of gushing blood and swollen eyes.

Tommy walked upstairs to the coffee shop and looked at the waitress who looked down at Tommy's blood dripping hands. She looked back at Tommy who winked at her and had a strange smile on his face, projecting to her he knows she is turned on by the sight of his bloody hands. Tommy exited the coffee shop and walked across the street to a bar. He went over to the corner of the bar, reached over, grabbed a bottle of whiskey and walked out. The bar tender seeing Tommy's wrapped bloody hands didn't say a word. Tommy took a swig and walked back across the street and went through the coffee shop and down the stairs into the basement where Granello is slumped in a corner, bleeding.

Tommy took another swig of whiskey and passed the bottle off to his muscle. When it came back around Tommy had one more snort from the bottle and bashed it over Granellos head. Granello begged Tommy for mercy.

"The more you beg, the worse its gonna get, *Sally*," Tommy said.

"Tommy … wait," Granello said coughing up blood.

"What did you say to the girls, when they would beg you to stop, *Sally*," Tommy said.

Tommy took the half of the bottle that broke off in his hand and rammed into Granello's crotch. He grinded and twisted it deeper into Granello as he whaled in agony.

"This is for the children you raped, you fat fucking scumbag," Tommy said as he pushed the shards of glass into Granello as hard as he could and left it there.

Granello fell to the ground and rolled over sideways. He was all screamed out and grew silent.

"You know what Sally, lets talk over some coffee. Maybe we can work something out," Tommy said.

Tommy looked at one his men.

"Go get us a fresh pot of coffee."

Tommy was handed a full pot of coffee.

"What? No cups?" Tommy asked.

Tommy then poured the whole scolding hot pot of coffee onto Granello's face. Bloodcurdling screams bellowed out of the bloody heap of what was left of Granello.

"You don't mind it black do you?" Tommy said

Tommy then pulled out a .44-Magnum and blasted Granello four times in the face.

"That's for being a rat," Tommy said to himself.

Granello's slain body was discovered on October 6, 1970 on the Lower East Side, and a December 16, 1970 FBI memo states:

> Detective Ray DRISCOLL, 7th Squad, New York City Police Department (NYCPD), advised October 6, 1970, that the Department had located an abandoned car on the East River Drive at Houston Street this date. A search of the vehicle revealed a body of a white male, matching the description of SALVATORE GRANELLO. The body was wrapped in heavy canvas or drop cloth with a green plastic wrapping about the head. * * * Detective DRISCOLL informed that an autopsy was being conducted as the body was in an advanced state of decomposition. According to DRISCOLL, bullet holes were observed in the skull of GRANELLO. Detective DRISCOLL advised that the autopsy report was not available, but the police estimate the death occurred about eight to ten days prior, due to the decomposition of the remains.

Although Tommy did not draw any heat from law enforcement or the Commission for torturing and killing Granello, the Commission was still looking to take Tommy out.

Silvio Eboli was born on St. Patrick's Day, 1971 in Fort Lee, New Jersey, an irony his superstitious Italian family did not miss. On the streets, Tommy and Patsy both pretended to be Irish for decades and now their grandson was paying the price.

Meanwhile, director Francis Ford Coppola had just begun to shoot the Mafia epic *The Godfather*. The Eboli's new son in-law Al Lettieri, was offered the role of Virgil "The Turk" Sollozzo, and had to ask Tommy for permission to be in the film prior to shooting.

That spring, Lettieri invited Al Pacino, James Caan and the rest of the cast to Patsy's house to see a real Mafia family up close.

When the door bell rang Patsy's daughter, Giovannina Bellino opened the front door. There was, Pacino, Caan, Producer Al Ruddy and others of the cast and crew. They went downstairs to the "family" room, which had a bar, a pool table and a dozen large silver trays of Italian cuisine set on some fold-out card tables.

Before their descent, they all went by Silvio's crib to look at the newest member of the Eboli family. Pacino leaned in close to get a look at Silvio and kissed his little hand like he was a don. Everyone in the room laughed before they drifted downstairs, follow-

Spring 1971: From left- Al Pacino, Patsy Eboli and Al Lettieri practicing Italian in Patsy's basement in Fort Lee, New Jersey days before filming *The Godfather* at Louis Restaurant in the Bronx.

ing the scent of eggplant Parmesan and other Italian dishes.

This night, when the real and celluloid Mafia first broke bread – only feet from Silvio's crib – has since become legend for those in the know of the untold history of Cosa Nostra.

In 2009, *Vanity Fair* published an article on this meeting between the Eboli family and *The Godfather* cast, but greatly embellished the whole event. Case in point, *Vanity Fair* reported that Marlon Brando was present at the dinner when in fact he was not.

"I was there that night and met everyone and Marlon Brando was definitely not there that night," one Eboli family insider told me.

"I was shocked that a magazine as respected as *Vanity Fair* could just publish any old BS they feel like whether its true or not" she continued.

After dinner, Patsy was given a copy of *The Godfather* script by Ruddy in order to consult Al Pacino later in the week. Pasquale took a liking to the tale of Michael Corleone, and how through his father's death, rises to become the family boss.

When Pacino arrived in Fort Lee a few weeks later, Patsy ran outside and paid the hungry, broke actor's cab fare, then asked his new wife Jean to whip up some linguine and clam sauce for him.

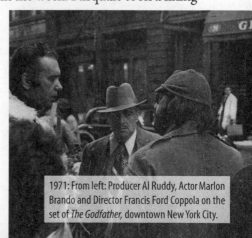

1971: From left: Producer Al Ruddy, Actor Marlon Brando and Director Francis Ford Coppola on the set of *The Godfather,* downtown New York City.

While they ate, Patsy, Pacino and Lettieri practiced their Italian for the crucial scene to be shot at Louis Restaurant in the Bronx later that week.

A few hours and wine bottles later, Pasquale, Pacino and Literati staggered into the backyard.

Patsy went back inside, picked up his new grandson and stumbled again out into the night. The two actors were still drifting outside, barely able to stand.

Patsy loudly sang the old Sicilian Mafia song "Blood Cries For Blood" into the moonlight, tears rolling down his face.

On the set of *The Godfather*, Patsy marveled at all that went into making a film. He coached Pacino through the Italian dialogue shot at Louis Restaurant. When one part of the script was too difficult for Pacino to recite, they shot it in English instead.

Coppola later recalled that the studio wanted to pull the plug on *The Godfather*, but after viewing the reels shot at the Louis Restaurant they were hooked and funded the rest of the film.

Louis Restaurant: From left- Actors Al Pacino, Sterling Hayden and Al Lettie[r]

On March 15, 1972, Patsy, Tommy and the rest of the Eboli clan went to *The Godfather's* world premiere at Lowes State Theater on 45 Street and 7th Avenue in Times Square. Patsy was entranced by *The Godfather's* operatic narrative and he went to see it many times when it was later released into wider circulation.

The Godfather went on to win Oscars for Best Picture, Best Actor – Marlon Brando – and Best Screenplay Adaption – Mario Puzo and Coppola. The sequel *The Godfather II*, also won an Oscar for Best Picture two years later in 1974.

The Godfather has over time become one of the most iconic films ever for both cinema fans and critics alike, weaving itself into American culture like no other film before or after. *The Godfather's* cult following has recently tipped the scales over *Citizen Kane* as the best movie ever made.

The Godfather is also the most important films shot in New York.

As the world became enthralled with the fictional Corleone family, Tommy and the Genovese crime family were falling apart. Tommy was spinning out of control, the drugs, the booze and the girls were taking all its toll.

At a 4th of July backyard barbecue of sausage and peppers in the Bronx, the Commission decided it was time to make a move on Tommy.

On July 16, 1972 at around 1AM, Tommy exited his girlfriend's apartment in Crown Heights, Brooklyn. His bodyguard and driver Joseph Sternfeld got out of the driver's side door and opened the back door for Tommy. Suddenly a red and white van pulled up and a .45 semi-automatic with an attached silencer leaned out the window. Before the trigger was pulled Tommy looked and saw his old fighter Gigante holding the gun that was pointed at him.

Five shots were pumped into his face as Tommy fell to the ground. His hand was scrambling to reach for a gold crucifix around his neck, but he was unable to before he died.

When police arrived at the scene they found Tommy slumped on the sidewalk, blood still oozing from his head. Sternfeld moved Tommy to make sure he was dead. Police took Sternfeld in as material witness. When he said he did not see the face of the man who killed Tommy, he was released the next morning. The red and white van and another stolen escape car were both found still

A bloodstained sidewalk and police chalk lines in front of 388 Lefferts Ave., Brooklyn, mark spot wher Mafia boss Thomas Eboli aka Tommy Ryan met his end. Eboi was shot five times while sitting in Caddy, slaggered from car and died. (Photo By: Frank Giorandino/NY Daily News via Getty Images)

running that night, but to this day, Tommy's murder is still unsolved.

The Eboli clan found out that Gigante was the trigger man, and he quickly replaced Tommy as head of the Genovese family. He later became known as the "Oddfather" for his faking to be insane in order to avoid prosecution.

Tommaso V. Eboli was buried in George Washington Memorial Park in Paramus, New Jersey. He was so hated in New York, only members of the Eboli family and law enforcement attended the funeral and burial services.

The Oddfather knew that Patsy was on guard after Tommy's murder and would be hard to get to. So he waited a few years before making a move.

In August 1976, Gigante believed the time was right to whack Patsy. A few weeks later Patsy disappeared. Police found Patsy's car in JFK airport's long term parking lot with the keys in the glove compartment. The police believe – and all that has since been published – contend that since Tommy was gunned down in the streets, it was more likely Patsy's killers buried him somewhere in the Catskills, possibly even in Swan Lake in honor of all those that he buried there. The car was left at JFK to muddy the waters, and give the appearance that Patsy had "disappeared."

But none of that is true and for the first time what really happened to Pasquale "Patsy" Eboli is finally revealed.

Patsy was tipped off about Gigante's hit soon after it was issued. According to family, Patsy – who was incredibly superstitious – experienced an apparition while visiting the Observation Deck after dinner and drinks in the Rainbow Room with a mistress and security.

As Patsy walked the boat like deck – one of the best views in NYC – an illuminating image of the Lady Of Guadalupe appeared over the skyline and warned him of Gigante's plans to kill him. Patsy dropped to his knees and did the sign if the cross. His security guard – nicked named "J.I. Joe" because he was formerly in the military – ran over thinking he was hit. When he picked Patsy up the Lady disappeared. J.I. Joe heard Patsy mutter "Africa?" under his breath as they lifted him up.

The next day, Patsy went back to Manhattan and ordered a large custom gold and diamond Lady of Guadalupe medallion. He also bought a new set of luggage, all filled with new clothes and left them at a mistress's apartment in Alden Manor by JFK airport.

On the eve of Patsy's escape he asked his wife, Jean, to make a big meal and invite the whole family over. At dinner he wore the Lady of Guadalupe chain, which everyone was blown away by.

The next day he told his family he was going to JFK to "meet somebody" and he did not want security crew to go along.

"That was suspicious in my mind," one family member told me. "J.I. Joe went everywhere with him."

Patsy also left the medallion behind – found in his desk by one of his daughters a few days

A never before published photograph of Patsy Eboli from the Eboli family's private collection. "From the way he dressed to how he carried himself, you would have never guessed Patsy was in the Mafia," said one Eboli family member.

after his disappearance, a twist that perplexed everybody in the Eboli clan even more.

What exactly did it all mean?

What the tight lipped Eboli clan did not tell police was that they hired a private detective to find out what had happened to Patsy.

According to what the Eboli clan uncovered, Patsy drove himself to JFK, parked his car at the airport and purchased a one way flight to Lagos International Airport in Nigeria. The ticket counter lady later recalled this to one of Patsy's daughters that she checked in several bags of Patsy's that were clearly "brand new."

The Eboli clan believes that from Lagos, Patsy, made his way to Tunisia and boated into Sicily, possibly with a fake passport. After Patsy disappeared, the Ebolis discovered that the family patriarch not only had several mistresses, but in fact several families. With that information, the Ebolis figured it all out. With the sociopathic ability to create new families, that is exactly what he did overseas and probably lived to an old age in the quiet rural hills of Sicily.

If Pasquale Eboli was still alive in 2015, he would be 91 years old.

Summer 2013; Author Toby Rogers at Golden Ratio Ranch, Paradise Valley, Montana.

CHAPTER FOUR

Pass The Dutchie

Stoned is the way of the walk ...
    – Cypress Hill

It took seven years for the Eboli clan to get a death certificate from New York state, since no body was ever recovered. In 1983 when Patsy's will was finally executed, the properties, stocks and horse stables were quickly liquidated and distributed among Patsy's family.

Written into his will a week before he disappeared, Patsy left Silvio the opulent Lady Of Guadalupe chain. Silvio put it in a guitar case, where it would stay for years at time, wearing it only on the most special of occasions.

In 1984, some of the Eboli clan had moved to Scarsdale, New York. They bought a successful fish store next to an old Tudor movie house on the edge of town. There Silvio, would unload, scale, gut and wrap fish for his uncles on the weekends.

That summer I walked in the fish store, asked about the "Help Wanted" sign and was hired on the spot to help unload the trucks that drove from Fulton Street Fish Market to the shop in the morning.

The Eboli clan still had a small piece of Fulton and got almost all of the fish they sold for free. I made $100 cash every day.

Six months later, Silvio invited me to a family party on Christmas Eve.

After a few eggnogs, I began to wonder: A cash-only fish store; engraved initials on the Cadillac doors matching the driver's sweat suit; gold watches and oversized rings; Frank Sinatra records; baked Ziti; large tin-foil trays of sausages and veal, and that shady poker game in the basement.

A sense of guilt set in. After all they have done for me, inviting me into their home – handing me a X-Mas card with a $1000 cash inside – how could I fall victim to such an awful Italian stereotype?

For our generation, the 1980's was a time of dystopia wedged between the Regan revolution and the ashes of Woodstock. We heard about the Chicago riots of 1968 through our aging hippie teachers wearing elbow padded blazers, acting as if *they* were actually there. It was continually drummed into our heads from both the left and right, that a great battle for social justice was fought and lost in the 1960's and that we were just living in its ruins.

We roamed the streets in ripped jeans and tattered overcoats our fathers wore out commuting to Wall Street and had thrown out. Mike Tyson, Suicidal Tendencies and flannel shirts. Bad Brains and dime bags from Gun Hill Road in the Bronx. The world we lived in was like old broken-down movie palace, coved in dust, yet still retaining some its opulent character. Even the wealthy and iconic village of Scarsdale had large abandoned buildings by the train station that we and several other gangs from Scarsdale and Eastchester valiantly fought over with brass knuckles, skateboards and switchblades. It was a time before security cameras and the Internet and where stickball in the streets was more fun than the primitive home video games like Atari or Asteroids at the pizza shop.

Edgewood at the time was considered the slum of Scarsdale. Hardly a slum, but compared to the other sections of the over the top wealthy village, it was. Unlike the rest of Scarsdale, there were hardly any Jews in Edgewood, and the ones that did live there sometimes suffered for it. They would get beat up and pennies would be thrown at them at school. It was where, working class Irish, Italians, Puerto Ricans and other minorities who had made a step up and moved, so their children would get a good education and assimilate with the other Edgewood upper class WASPS.

Besides the Eboli clan, Edgewood had a few other Irish mob families, but they only committed low-level fire department and construction hustles.

In 1985, Silvio started playing bass, practicing for hours every day.

For Silvio, the summer of 1985 was a pivotal year. He lost his virginity, decided to become a musician and most importantly, it was when he first got high on weed. He first smoked it the basement of his friend Mark Dann in the "Edgewood" section of Scarsdale.

Dann was the best technical guitar player in Scarsdale and had three older brothers, two much older. One time Dann's older brother smoked him out and he turned all of us on to weed. Part of Dann's basement had been converted into a sound proof jam room, where his teen aged trio would play the Dammed, U2 (before Joshua Tree) and Jimi Hendrix. The basement had its own entrance from the garage, which was at the bottom of a steeply curved driveway. Mark and Silvio built a skate board ramp, which they would hit at full velocity at the bottom of the driveway. Mark would also buy beer with his brother's ID, usually 40oz of Old English or Private Stock.

In the mid-80's, Dann's basement was just about the coolest place in Scarsdale.

I lived right behind the Danns and would regularly hang out with them. There was always kids around, mostly hoodlums from Edgewood and the Bronx, in a circle taking bong hits while listing to Anthrax. It was a plastic bong that was red green and gold. The room always smelled like bong-water, since it had been spilled on the rug endless times.

We were surrounded by life-sized Hendrix posters, and smaller ones of Eddie Van Halen and Stevie Ray Vaughn cut out of *Guitar Magazine*. There was also a small black and white picture of John Coltrane that stood in stark contrast to the rest of the artwork on the wall. The ceiling was covered with an orange and blue Indian cloth.

John Coltrane

One time I remember, everybody was laughing uncontrollably and I could not figure out what was so funny since they weren't saying anything.

"Kunta" Dann sneered at me, "Take a hit."

"I'm cool," I said, "No thanks"

"You are taking it a hit Kunta." Dann said, "If you don't, we are gonna kick your ass."

"Just toke already, stop being such a wuss." Silvio bellowed.

I reluctantly agreed.

I remember not being able to move for hours, until someone poured beer on me.

During the 1980s, the Japanese population began to explode in Scarsdale.

In 1986, Morihei E. and his parents had just moved from Japan into a quaint Dutch-Colonial that was close to Scarsdale High School. He was determined to become "Mr. Popularity" just as he had been in Tokyo and decided to throw an open house party. Posing as his father, he ordered a keg of Heineken over the phone, and had it delivered to the house Saturday afternoon.

When Silvio's and Dann's band, Utopia, was setting up in the living room, a few things broke by accident. Morihei was down stairs in the garage minding the keg, where kids threw darts and smoked weed. Upstairs the dinning room was jammed with kids as well as the living room. Cigarette butts piled up.

I went down stairs and got four cups of beer for the band and myself. We went out on the porch. Silvio lit a joint. "Its gonna be a wild night," he said as the joint was passed around.

That turned out to be an understatement. As Utopia jammed, the darts began to be thrown at other things on the wall like the swordfish and paintings. The dining room table was getting scratched and damaged by kids dancing on it. You could feel in it the air. Everybody knew that by the end of the night that house was going to get very fucked up.

We walked into to Morihei's father's office and looked around its walls. On it were dozens of pictures of himself in Japan.

Then we saw it.

A framed picture of Morihei's father with Ronald Reagan in the Oval Office. Reagan, in our young minds, was the personification of evil. Our parents may have voted for the old fuck, but the 1980s youth culture looked at him as if he was Frankenstein.

I took the picture off the wall and brought it to the stage as the song ended. I held it in front of everyone. Everyone looked horrified and turned to Morihei.

Dann took off for second to fill his cup. I took the picture and set it on fire with a lit candle from the living room mantle. Everybody roared in approval. I pick up Dann's guitar and cranked the volume. Silvio and I and the drummer play pure noise feedback at ear splitting volumes. The party goers proceed to smash the shit out of everything in sight.

Vases flew in the air, bodies surfed on the dining table, pitchers of beer were dumped on computers and other electronics – a whirlwind of destruction engulfed every square inch of the place.

Dann came back and grabbed the guitar out of my hand. I looked behind him and see two jocks about to toss a swordfish like a javelin at us.

"Get down."

We all ducked as the aquatic creature sailed over us. It slammed into the wall behind us. When we got up we couldn't stop laughing. Mark started the intro to "Let The Good Times Roll."

I found a bag of golf clubs and handed them out to everyone in sight. Like a demolition crew – we all went to work. The stair bannister crashed down. Some others started a fire in the fireplace, with smashed paintings and sofa cushions. In the kitchen the refrigerator was tipped over with the doors spread open on the floor. Unopened Coors Light cans glowed red in the microwave, twirling around on the little plate.

Mayhem eclipsed all floors I ran into the living room and grabbed the mike from the stand and scraped it across the low note strings of an open grand piano. It created a loud screeching effect that boomed over all the other musicians. Silvio burst out laughing and put his guitar down. He moved his amp and picked up a glass coffee table and threw it through the main living room window. The glass shattered and burst into crystals. The noise was operatic. Silvio and I ran upstairs where the football team was taking apart the master bedroom. While they focused on the stomping the wooded bed frame, Silvio and I found a safe full of cash and jewelry. We grabbed the loot and went out the porch door on the top floor.

Outside we saw Silvio's bass-amp roll into the pool along with the drums and the grand piano, which had been set ablaze.

Then the cops rolled up. We both grabbed onto a tree branch extending over the porch.

"Kunta, go shut the door" Silvio ordered.

I went over and shut it. Squad cars poured in from every direction. We climbed up the tree as far as we could. We hid for hours until the pigs split. Just before dawn we slithered down the tree and hid the money and jewelry on the roof of Scarsdale High School, smoking a joint while the sun rose.

"We must have about $8,000 in cash and a few thousand in jewelry," Silvio estimated.

We got hauled in by the Scarsdale Police a few days later, but they couldn't do shit since Morihei had bought and supplied us with the beer, and we were underage. Silvio and I split the cash, took the loot to "Uncle Frank" Eboli, and he sold it off for us

Silvio quickly replaced his lost equipment, and I bought an arsenal of fireworks from Chinatown. We spent the rest of the summer terrorizing Scarsdale. We would tape M-80s – real M-80s that were advertised as an 1/8 of a stick of dynamite – on the largest panes of the largest windows we could find and blow them out. Our local town paper, the *Scarsdale Inquirer*, described our nights blowing up Scarsdale as a "Wave Of Vandalism."

It was remarkable we never got caught.

Silvio continued to practice bass religiously. We all played a little, but he took it much more seriously than all of us. When he heard Jaco Pastorius, he became obsessed.

Jaco Pastorius.

Soon Silvio wanted a fret-less base too, like Pastorius. He gutted and scaled fish at the shop on the weekends, but it still was not enough.

Silvio started jamming with an older musician, Chico from the city, when one day he saw him pull out some weed behind his amplifier. Then he saw Chico's money roll.

Silvio wanted in.

"You could mule for me if you want," Chico said, "$4,000 a trip."

His first trip to Jamaica was rough. "I was a nervous wreck the whole time. When they pulled me over to check something my heart stopped," Silvio said.

By his third run, he knew where all the best bars, restaurants and girls were from Kingston to Negril.

Silvio fell in love with Jamaica, its rich culture, traditions and music. He also had more time and money to fuel his band, which he formed with his two cousins.

They had gotten few gigs in some dives around the Lower East Side. Silvio musically eclipsed his cousins, and everyone he knew told him to cut them loose. But Silvio struggled on with them even though his family dragged him down. Silvio booked all the gigs and coordinated all the logistics, while his cousins basically showed up to complain. Getting them to practice a few times a week was almost impossible. All his cousins did was bitch and moan about everything.

Silvio marched on with them regardless. Why he endured their antics was even beyond him. He wanted to make it in the music business, and he wanted his cousins along for the ride. Like many rappers with large posse's of family and friends. And like any good Italian, he was trying to keep the family together.

As much as the band frustrated Silvio, when everything clicked, he was ecstatic. Much of the time the music was secondary to the antics off stage.

Yet, overall Silvio's life could not have been better. He had more money and got laid much more than a kid his age should. He worked only a few days a month, which required him to fly to Jamaica, jam at reggae clubs and party on some of the dopest beaches in the Caribbean.

Over time, Silvio looked forward to flying to Jamaica to experience its rich culture. He started playing bass for a few reggae acts which also gave more cover to mule.

Silvio soon dropped out of school, moved to Manhattan and started earning $250 a day delivering weed as a "bike, messenger."

A few years later, in 1992, Silvio met Chris Farley at a party and quickly made him and others in the *Saturday Night Live* cast and crew clients.

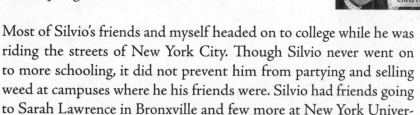

Chris Farley

Most of Silvio's friends and myself headed on to college while he was riding the streets of New York City. Though Silvio never went on to more schooling, it did not prevent him from partying and selling weed at campuses where he his friends were. Silvio had friends going to Sarah Lawrence in Bronxville and few more at New York University, Hunter College and Columbia University in Manhattan.

Silvio also liked Bennington College, where I was going and drove up from the city quite frequently, starting in the fall of 1993 to see Fugazi play on campus. Silvio was drawn to Bennington for its rural isolation and eccentric, artistic vibe.

Bennington was also where Silvio could unload a lot of weed at once. He would get up to campus four or five times a semester, generously giving me a cash cut each time. Because of the lopsided "progressive" female/male student body ratio, Silvio always got laid when he chilled at Bennington.

That fall on October 1, 1993, a campus band named Hagit was holding an mushroom induced "art party" in the red brick recreation room. It took a while for the hallucinogens to kick in, but when they did none of us were ever the same after that night. It felt like wave of energy drifted into the room from outside. Other musicians that were tripping – some on mushrooms, others on LSD – had brought instruments with them and joined in. It eventually turned into a epic four-hour tribal jam of noise-rock and free-jazz improvisation. Hagit's lead singer Keith was in a trance, dancing and chanting around room, wearing an American flag around his neck. When he took off the flag and began to dance on the it, the locals behind the bar jumped in and a fight almost broke out. Keith was more interested in the music

Above: October 1, 1993: Hagit poster- Mushroom/Acid party at Bennington College, Bennington, Vermont. Below: Hagit lead singer Keith Reynolds.

"People, you are playing earth chords, I need space chords," Keith boomed into the mike, "space chords, space chords, space muthafuckas! Lets take it into space!"

Horns wailed on pure overtones, drums pounded and guitars slung feedback from crackling Marshall stacks for hours. There were musicians from every part of the globe, North and South America,

Africa, India, the Middle East, Europe and Asia all tripping, all jamming in the language of music, in ways and sounds never heard before, yet at the same time, it felt archaically ancient.

Silvio brought large jar of potent liquid acid he bought in Brooklyn. He was dosing everybody for $15 a drop, when Keith knocked Silvio over and spilled acid all over both of them. It also splashed on everybody around them. Keith got soaked the worst, his hair, neck and shoulders were saturated.

At first Silvio passed out, but awoke hours later outside a bonfire at the "end of the world," as the edge of campus overlooking the mountains was called by students.

"Sil," guitarist Jean Paul Jenkins yelled in his ear, "We played the acid, man!, we rode the acid!"

"I'm still riding bro," Silvio said in daze.

"So am I man! So am I," Jenkins said, laughing hysterically.

Silvio heard the drums pounding by the fire. The jam had marched its way outside, all the way to the end of the world. The bonfire raged. Keith was still dancing with the American flag, then he handed it off to a red-headed topless hippie girl. She danced under the moonlight and stars that illuminated the darkness on the surrounding hills. When she whirled, her hair and the red and white stripes trailed off like visual vibrations.

Keith finally sat down by the fire next to Silvio, a bottle of whiskey in his hand. He passed it off to Silvio.

"We started a new religion tonight. A new religion for a new millennium, of mushrooms and weed and drums and revolution," Reynolds said, "and rebirth. And *She* is going to spread all over the world from here and into space."

The sun began to rise, hitting the fall foliage in an explosion of light.

"A new dawn is rising," Keith told Silvio, who was clutching Patsy's gold chain around his neck. Silvio took off the chain and held it in the sunlight. There the golden Lady of Guadalupe, which Patsy Eboli had worn only once and left behind, looked like she was dancing. Silvio handed the Lady to Keith, who raised Her over his head as the sun peeked over the mountain.

"Here She is," Keith said to us all out of his mind on acid, "a dancing Goddess to show us the way."

Both Silvio and Keith tripped all weekend and into Monday, while the rest of us sobered up after breakfast and slept the rest of the day.

For the next twenty years, every time a major social uprising took place around the world Keith would contact me. It started with the Zapatista uprising in Chiapas, Mexico on new years day 1994, then six years later after the "Battle in Seattle" at the end of 1999. Four years later in February of 2003 – when protests around the world erupted against Bush's unilateral invasion of Iraq – and again on election night 2008, when Barack Obama won, Keith called me out of the blue. In 2011, Keith called me several times, when Tunisia, Egypt and Libya's dictators all fell and again on October 1, 2011, when the Occupy Movement tents sprouted up just about everywhere around the world. Each time Keith would call and say the same thing.

You see, its spreading. She is spreading around the world, just like I said it would at Bennington.

The following Christmas eve, Silvio was walking through downtown Manhattan when he saw Vincent Gigante staggering down the street in a bathrobe with two bodyguards on each side of him. Silvio followed for a couple of blocks until they reached Sullivan Street. There the Oddfather disappeared into a building.

Silvio tried to find Gigante again, hanging around Sullivan Street from time to time. But he never saw Gigante again, who later was

Vincent Gigante aka "The Oddfather," downtown New York City.

picked up and sent to prison until his death on December 19, 2005.

After graduating from Bennington 1996, I moved to Los Angeles and later to Texas. But soon I was back in New York in 1998 and Silvio got me a job at a bagel shop in Scarsdale. For years he had used the shop as a front to sell weed. The kid he had in there, Miles, over the course of ten years had degraded into a full blown junkie and was royally fucking up in every way possible.

When Miles dozed off driving to work and crashed into another car, Silvio moved me from the morning shift to Miles' afternoon shift. I also had to take care of the special side-orders. If a customer asked for two nonexistent "pumpernickel everything" I would pack a $50 bag of weed from a backpack that one of Silvio's cousins would drop off to me each day.

Silvio paid me $150 off the top, plus I was allowed to take bud when ever I wanted. Over time merchants on the street would give me free stuff out of respect. I didn't get it totally, even though it was right under my nose.

I was working for Cosa Nostra.

In 1997, Silvio's girlfriend, Leah — a stunning blond Israeli model — was hired as a "market analyst" at Bernard L. Madoff Investment Securities. Silvio had first met Madoff at Leah's first office Christmas party held at the Montauk Yacht Club on Long Island.

Bernie Madoff

Silvio was struck with how soft spoken Madoff was. He barely moved, yet was still able to charm everybody in the room.

Before Silvio plated up at the football field length seafood bar, he went out to the docks to light up.

Mark Madoff, Bernie's son, asked Silvio if he may join in. Mark asked Silvio if he could buy some weed. Silvio agreed and later discovered that the purchase was for Bernie himself.

When Silvio got back inside, he saw Madoff standing very close to Leah. He walked over and stood between them and smiled. Madoff looked at Silvio like he was a leper.

Leah introduced Silvio to Madoff. Silvio extended his hand out to Madoff and was left hanging. Madoff looked Silvio up and down, turned around, took Leah by the hand and walked away with her.

Madoff had only one thing in mind when he hired Leah, he wanted to fuck her. And he was not interested in a love triangle, wanting Leah all to himself.

Silvio stepped up his game and took Leah on trips to Jamaica, Cuba, Barbados, Nevis, Argentina, Paris, London, Morocco and Spain.

Silvio also started seeing a gorgeous, wealthy Bollywood actress on the side, just in case Leah ever dumped him for Madoff.

But in the summer of 2001, Leah found out she was pregnant with Silvio's child.

Bike messenger, New York City.

CHAPTER FIVE

The Rise of
The Ganja Godfather

Guess who's back, no longer trapped
Cuz, I snapped on the ones that held me back
— Tupac Shakur

As the summer sun blazed down on the streets of lower Manhattan, the muggy heat and the cumbersome backpack of pot strapped to Silvio's shoulders blazed through another day. Biking from customer to customer, block to block, the endless stomp up stairway after stairway for eight hours in 90 degree heat was more than exhausting.

It was deadly.

His only escape was the music in his portable CD player – Bonga-Angola 1972.

At all times Silvio had to remain focused. For one lapse, even a split second of distraction – a hot babe in tight jeans or even a two foot blue Mohawk on some punk-rock wannabe – could cause a whole litany of potential accidents ranging anywhere from mowing down a trembling old lady with a cart of groceries to a head on collision with a city bus.

It had happened many times before to other drivers, usually resulting in broken limbs of some kind. One Irish kid named Jim was slammed from the side by a drunken off duty cop and was killed almost instantly.

What happens when a drunk cop slams into a pot dealer on a bike? When Jim and his backpack slammed on to the sidewalk and dozens of plastic boxes each containing $50 of weed spilled out, before anyone could even think of calling 911, Jim's stash, money and cell phone had vanished.

The overwhelming majority of accidents were always in the summer.

Silvio was not going out like that. He loved his life too much. During these hot days, he tried not to think, not to focus on his suffering, or even daydream, just peddle, and keep an eye on what's ahead.

It was the third straight week of scorching heat. Hour after hour, day after day, the sweat and aching muscles were like a whirlwind of pain which Silvo tried to just block out. He was earning $250 a day, tax free.

Silvio would see his comrades riding across the way, but they never waved or acknowledged each other.

Until July 4, 2001.

It started after nightfall. For the first time, bike messengers started being robbed. First was Sneakers on Houston Street and then Paulie at University Place. Of the six riders out on July 4th who were tagged, two were taken down inside a five-minute window.

Silvio, head dispatcher radioed his riders. "Yo, everybody meet at Astor Place now."

When they all arrived, they huddled around Silvio who was standing in front of the cube. Whenever a crisis erupted all eyes turned to Silvio, and oddly enough he always figured a way out.

"What the fuck, any of you seen this before?" Silvio asked rhetorically.

"Never. Totally fucking new." said Gums

"Oh shit," said Beastie, looking over Silvio's shoulder, where about ten thugs rolled in.

The Alamo aka "The Cube," outdoor sculptur by Bernard (Tony) Rosenthal, New York City.

Silvio knew they had penetrated their communications. How else would they know where and when to attack.

"We're gonna fly down Saint Marks Street in a line, full speed. I don't care what's in front of you. We split up in Tompkins Square and meet back in McSorley's on 7th. Got it?" Silvio said.

They jumped on their bikes and raced down Saint Marks. As they got closer to Tompkins Square Park, fireworks erupted overhead, lights flashed explosions boomed. The crowd on Saint Marks was heavy but thinned as they got closer to the park. Silvio turned around and saw the goons were nowhere in sight.

When they reached the park they scattered. The fireworks dancing overhead. Silvo banked right and glided by a pack of Hare Krishna's singing and dancing around a tree. By then all he could hear was Miles Davis' *Bitches Brew*. He had been playing the CD since Astor Place. After 10 years of biking weed around Manhattan Silvio had become as mentally steeled as any ancient Samurai warrior. He knew like just any true warrior in battle that death looms behind every shadow and his life could alter or cease with every ticking second.

As they each looped around to McSorley's, Silvio was stressed. With their cover blown it was not safe to ride.

McSorley's Ale House, a living historical landmark from the 19th Century.

While Silvio and crew sat at McSorley's – the "black stone" of the Lower East Side – he realized it was someone on the inside, possibly even sitting at the table.

He called the boss, the "Chief" from the Irish mob.

"We've been infiltrated Chief. I don't know what you want to do, but we can't operate like this. This wasn't planned well from the get. Its a holiday, everybody is in the streets, Bush in town," Silvio said

"I agree. Tomorrow come in with everyone's tickets and we'll talk. I'm sending you out of town tomorrow night. Have your passport with you, " Chief said.

"You got it Chief." Silvio said back. A smile broke across his face as he slammed the phone down.

"Jamaica", Silvio said to himself. He could not wait to get out of Manhattan that night and lay on the beaches of Negril.

The next morning, Silvio woke up and lit a spliff. He grabbed a coffee and cabbed over to the office. Chief was already there and ... on edge.

"I don't fucking get it, Silvio. We pay you guys good money just to bike around the city. And this shit happens."

"It's n-e-v-e-r happened to me before, Chief. Somebody inside let them in."

"I was told it was you."

"You know that's bullshit Chief."

"Today I'm firing everybody. In two weeks, we will set up shop again. Meanwhile you are going to Negril and bring back some weight OK?"

"Sure."

"These fucking punks Silvio. They are fucking everything up! They have no honor, even a dog has honor Sil. They are worse than dogs."

"Where did you find them Chief, all the customers complain."

"I know I know. They always ask for you Sil. *Mr. Scarsdale.*"

"We are going to their home. They don't know these guys. They roll up all thugged. They look like they'd rob their own mother."

"Can you get people?"

"Maybe. Not while I'm Negril."

"That's going to take three days."

"No it is not. Nobody goes to Jamaica for three days. I'll be searched." Silvio jokes. "You trying to set me up?"

"Yeah, with a ten-pound cash order. I just gotta get back in operation fast. I'm losing a lot of money."

"Ten pounds?" Silvio said shocked, "That's a lot for one trip."

"This run will make or break this delivery business."

"... I hear you Chief."

Two days later Silvio flew in to Negril just before sunset. He threw his bags down and went on the porch to make a call to Sami Jo. Her name was Samantha Josephine. She was nineteen and had the thickest booty on the island. Her father, who owned the largest new and used car franchise in the Caribbean, was contracted by the government to supply all the police their vehicles on the whole island. He is also the Jamaica's largest coke and ganja smuggler.

"Sami Jo? It's Sil."

"Heeeyyy baby, what u doin?"

"I'm at the hotel."

"Soon come … about 10 minutes."

That meant an hour or two. So Silvio took a shower and waited for Sam at the hotel bar.

When Sami Jo entered the bar, her huge hips and long thick dreadlocks put everyone in a trance. She walked over to Silvio and gave him a hug. After a few shots of rum, they went upstairs, partied and fucked all night.

The next morning, Silvio watched the sun rise over the ocean. The hotel room's view of the beach was stellar. As the salty air breezed in, the smell of ganja and cigar paper trickled out the window.

After one more ball, Silvio and Sami got down to business.

Silvio told Sami, " I need ten."

"Strapped on you?"

Silvio nodded yes.

"You crazy Silvio!" Sami shot back. " You never gonna get through JFK with ten."

"Yes I will." Silvio explained. "I've done this so many times. What's an extra few pounds?"

"Its too fucking much, I'm telling you for real."

Sam drove Silvio up into the hills in her jeep. They soon got to the garden. "It must have been twelve acres", Silvio later recalled.

As they waded deep into the garden, with hundreds of ten-feet high plants, Sami tossed a blunt to Silvio and began to strip. Silvio took out his digital camera and took pictures.

Ganja Field, Jamaica.

"I love the smell of a ganja garden. It's like Jah is all around us."

"Its heaven on earth," Silvio replied.

"Then don't leave Silvio. Stay ... in the garden with me."

"I wish I could baby."

They kept walking through the ganja field until they reached a private bay. They sat and smoked a spliff. Silvio knew Sami Jo was right, ten pounds of weed was too much to mule. His silence did not stop his mind from screaming that fact to himself. He tried to enjoy the view and Sami 's dark ripe double D's and pear shaped booty. Maybe he should stay after all. As the waves slapped the shore, his mind drifted to an alternative life that would never be.

After two weeks of chilling in Negril, Silvio never felt better. He was happy Chief had to shut down. Sami really grew on him, as did the culture and the island mindset. He loved having a late breakfast with Sami on the beach, how she bopped around in her underwear, with a blunt always on her lips and a devilish gaze peering through her beautiful brown eyes.

On Silvio's final day, he sat with Sami all afternoon at a sea-side bar. Reggae tunes softly floated through the evening breeze.

"You know Silvio, one day Babylon will get you. And when they do, you are going to look back at this week and say to yourself. 'Sami Jo was right. I could be eating mangos and rumcakes by the beach, but instead I'm in jail .... for money."

Silvio reflected. "Your probably right. *I hope your wrong.* But I don't plan to be a mule my whole life."

"Oh I know you won't, Jah has bigger plans ahead for you."

At the hotel. Sami carefully taped ten pounds of weed around Silvio shins and thighs. Sami double wrapped the ganja.

At Kingston airport, Silvio sailed through.

But at JFK Silvio got busted, just like Sam said he would. Airport Security held him for a few hours then let him go. Keeping the bud – of course.

Silvio contacted Chief.

"What! Are you fucking kidding me? You got busted?"

"They got me Chief, I don't know what happened."

"Now I'm out for another two weeks," he said.

In mid-August Chief sent Sivio down to Negril again, this time the mule hired other mules.

After Labor Day, Chief is back in full glory – everything was back to normal. He had to borrow some here and there, but his revenue stream was flowing again. Chief was looking forward to the holidays. Business always picks up then, and soon he would be back on top.

But then on September 11th, 2001, for the third and final time, Chief got buried – literally. Silvio was in Little Italy when the attacks occurred. By noon Chief's office, located in a basement by the World Trade Center, was covered in debris from the falling towers.

2001: 9/11- Downtown, New York City.

While Silvio watched the towers fall, he knew instantly that things in the pot-delivery business would change, possibly forever. Chief knew it also, especially after eating ten tickets. He did not want to be rescued with weed all over the basement office. He decided then and there that he needed a vacation for a few weeks, and mule himself a few pounds, then open back up when everything settles.

By noon the office – located in an basement apartment too close to the Twin Towers – was buried in debris.

Messengers simply scattered with their tickets. Silvio had 40 valued at $50 each, totaling $2000, and a key to Chief's large hidden stash. But he had something else, which was much more valuable. Silvio knew the client "list." Hell, he had had it memorized for years.

When the towers fell, Silvio sensed a rare opportunity. Chief would not be the only dog down – somebody would eventually fill the void in the pot-delivery business. While looking at the short term, folks would be positioning themselves better for the long term. He could see it all in his mind. The numbers, the bricks, scales and the profit margins floated through his frontal lobe after the weed he just smoked settled in. It was all right there in front of him. Like any visionary CEO, he just had to make it happen.

After all the years of muling and biking through Manhattan in the scorching summer heat, Silvio would finally be his own boss.

A few days later, Silvio biked downtown as far he could. He wanted to see how the police and the military would react to a messenger on a bike. He was surprised to see that they did nothing. He serendipitously had two tickets, which he thought he left behind.

Silvio thought of dumping them, when a client walked up to him and asked him if he had any "boxes," selling them on the spot.

Soon other clients were bumping into him on the streets as well – begging him for weed.

Within a week, word got around: Silvio has taken over.

Word also soon got around to Madoff that Leah was pregnant.

When Madoff heard the news his fragile ego snapped, lashing out at Leah after calling her to his office.

"I just gotta know one thing. What are you doing with that fucking hippie? You could of had gold. You could of had me. You could have had an apartment, a car, a driver. But instead you throw that all away for some fucking hippie!" Madoff bellowed.

Madoff's outburst triggered Leah to call in sick. She and Silvio drove to Cape Cod and eloped.

"The first few weeks after 9/11 were really touch and go," Silvio later recalled at the 21 Club. "It was hand to mouth for a little while. But in just one month, cash started flowing in."

By mid October 2001, Silvio felt on top of the world, pulling in anywhere from $3000 to $5000 a day.

At the end of that month, I got a call from Silvio out of nohwhere asking if I wanted to join him at Atlantic City with a few old friends of ours. I agreed and we all drove to New Jersey on Devil's Night.

As we drove, Silvio got a message from his old boss, "Chief":

> Yeah, I haven't heard from you guys, and this is turning into a big flake. I'm gonna come down there, you guys are gonna call up here, and we are going to figure this thing out right now. What happened is, property of mine is gone, there's nothing here for it and I need it. Today. I need resolution. Money. You don't grab things and finger them up. My customer service department is not functioning. I am not functioning right now on a normal level. So if you want to bring a bunch of guys that might be a good idea. I want my money and if I'm not getting it, I'm getting a whole lot else man, and maybe a piece of your fucking health.

The Chief made another call and left another message.

> Bill, this is the Chief, I'm giving you a ring. Its Halloween night, um I think I need you to do me a favor and get in contact with the Dukester. Tell 'em that I need a crew over at West Village, we're gonna roll over some white suburban punks who think there badass, but we all know they got pussies instead of cocks. Give me a call here as soon as you get this message and lets organize this.

The Chief hung up and went on a tirade, his assistant secretly taping him the whole time for Silvio.

> And Silvio's girlfriend too will get involved in that I'll have her beat shitless. You gotta go after the people that are dear to them. I'm the wrong PTSD psychopath motherfucker to fuck around with like this. Look at this I would have weed right now if I didn't have money I'd have something! Kathleen gave me a double dose of anti psychotic medication look how good it did. $300,000 fucking dollars man!
>
> My money. Every fucking dime I have. I don't have a way to buy myself shit, right now, a fucking "Happy Meal."
>
> I'm killing some-fucking-body!

"Easy Boss easy," the Chief's assistant responded.

I do need to take it out on you as a matter of fact. This is your fuck up! My property is stolen, it's fucking stolen. It's gone .... And now you got friends involved that are gonna get fucking stabbed up like that.... I'm gonna rip his fucking face with that knife right there... Fuck with me.

"OK. Boss ... I'm with you here ... just calm down a little," the assistant said.

No. I haven't been giving the stimuli to calm down. I put the word and the vibes out there, and all I get is ignorance back. Nobody is contacting me. Nobody is reaching out as a matter of fact they are fucking laughing right now, they think I'm some fucking punk to be fucked with.

Silvio looked a his cell right before we walked into the Trump Marina casino. Then he listened to voice mail and said calmly.
"We gotta go."
As we burned down the New Jersey Turn Pike, Silvio called Leah over and over.
"Hey baby, please hit me back as soon as you get this. I'm heading home now," Sivio said into Leah's voice mail.
As we gunned over the George Washington Bridge, Silvio frantically hit redial over and over. Finally Leah picked up.
"Hey, I want you to get into a cab and meet me at the Marriott in Tarrytown."
"For real?" She asked.
"Yes," Silvio said
When we made it to Manhattan, Silvio jumped out at Times Square.
I'll call you tomorrow." Silvio yelled as he ran off. The Marriott in Tarrytown was code for Leah cab over to Grand Central Station, hop into another cab to the Hotel Iroquois on West 44th, only two blocks away.
Silvio shot through Times Square and made a right onto West 44th. He ran through lobby bypassing the line. The front desk lady handed him a room key and whispered the number.

Silvio walked in a found Leah – who looked more pregnant than ever to Silvio – sitting in the dark with a gun pointed at him. When he turned on the light, and Leah saw it was him, she started crying.

The next morning Silvio and Leah drove up to Saranac Lake in the Adirondacks. He rented a small cabin outside of town adjacent to old barbecue and lobster shack from the 1920's. From there he found another rental cabin for a few more weeks.

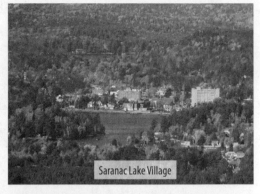
Saranac Lake Village

They drove around western New York as well, and Silvio met members of the Oneida Nation, who ended up becoming a really solid wholesale cannabis connection for years. He would meet them on the St. Lawrence river in canoes or on hiking paths along the shore.

"It was mostly "indica" trucked across the country from Vancouver, then across the St. Lawrence Seaway, or Lake Erie. The first time I did this, I couldn't believe it. It's totally dark, you couldn't see ten feet. Then out of fog come these Indians … Indians, in canoes, paddling, like right out of the fucking *Last of the Mohicans*, bringing in the weed."

For years, Silvio would drive upstate and bring product down from Canada through his Native American friends. They had a deep respect for each other, which grew over time.

"The Indians upstate never screwed me over," Silvio said, "They are they only ones."

Silvio laid low, refusing to meet the Chief, and he was not going to pay anything for the list – worth about $100,000 or more. The Chief had no sway with his clients either, who for the most part sided with Silvio.

So things were at a stand-still. And each day Silvio sold without the Chief's "blessing" was another day whereby the Chief lost his claim.

Over time, it appeared to simply fade away.

Contact between Silvio and I broke down during the Bush years, until I heard from him in 2009. From the September 2001 to 2009, Silvio had steadily built up his business to where he wanted.

By the end of the "00's," Silvio was quite a successful high-end weed dealer, pulling in anywhere from $50,00 to $100,000 a day, five days a week. He had five family members delivering weed on Vespas downtown. His Uncle Frank, the Eboli clan's patriarch, ran a huge distribution operation on the Upper West Side and bought all his bud from Silvio. The only customers Silvio directly dealt with were celebrities and NY's ultra elite.

Silvio also had someconstruction hustles downtown. He and his production crew would also regularly fleece a billionaire's wife, who on her spare time had built a performance space in midtown for wedding and other public events. She gave Silvio access to her credit cards, with which they purchased tons of production equipment. They'd steal it and rebuy everything again right under the old lady's nose, who was so rich she never even looked at her credit card accounts.

Madoff, on the other hand, eventually ended up with 150 years behind bars for fraud, becoming the media's greatest pariah since George W. Bush.

It was at this time Silvio was approached by *New York Magazine* about a profile. When the story was published, Silvio was disappointed, but not surprised. Silvio hadn't trusted Jacobs enough to tell him his whole story anyway, and after it ran, called me to reboot it, and "get the story right."

Chapter Six

Ghosts of Swan Lake

The snakes, the grass, too long, to see.
The lawnmower, sitting, rightnext, to the tree.
— DMX

As agreed, I shadowed Silvio for about six weeks. We were going to fly out to California to meet with his "cousins" out in Mendocino. "We are going to the 'Million Dollar Corner' out west," Silvio informed me. "You'll love San Fran and Mendocino. They got the best strip clubs in the country."

"The Million Dollar Corner?"

"It's in a small town called Ukiah," Silvio said.

The last time Silvio went, "I had $25,000 in my suitcase, and some friends tell me to drive up toward Ukiah, to the Million Dollar Corner — 'cause like a million dollars is changing hands there, like, every other day."

At the last minute, Silvio's plans changed when a new supplier emerged in the West Village, saving Silvio the trip to California, and raising his profit margin considerably

The Gay Mafia, aka "The Pink Hand," had decided to diversify their revenue stream, investing profits from gay porn into growing bud in San Francisco and setting up a underground wholesale shop in New York.

Silvio got a tip from a client with AIDS about the operation, and through him set up a meeting.

After buying a hundred pounds of high quality Sour Diesel at shwag prices, Silvio celebrated by taking a few friends and his little brother to Atlantic City for a 48-hour strip club marathon. Silvio also scored some backstage passes for U2 at Giant Stadium, which was about as exciting staring at a gray wall.

Silvio and I went to his house after the weekend in New Jersey. Being away for some time, Silvio's kids were happy to see him and crawled all over him. Leah walked over from her study and they embraced.

After a night watching Silvio at the Borgata Hotel tripping on mushrooms in a Jacuzzi with a handful of call girls from a New Jersey escort agency, it was odd to see him with his wife and kids, playing the perfect suburban dad.

Not for Silvio. This was just the way life was. He walked in with roses, a new gray cashmere sweater in a boutique box, a few $200 bottles of 1997 Ornellaia Bolgheri Superiore from Tuscany as well as freshly cut pasta, meatballs and sausages from a local Italian specialty market.

"I'll cook tonight," Silvio said to Leah, who wouldn't let go of him for the sweater and wine.

Leah explained that Italian wines from 1997 are "exceptionally good vintages, no matter what region in Italy the grapes were grown in that year."

Leah then apologized for the "dreadful condition of the kitchen." I looked around and realized what she meant. It was like a time capsule from the late 1950s: a bright plastic yellow with silver, chrome post-art-deco edges. Silvio had resisted remodeling of the house, not because he was cheap – he had people that would gladly do it for free – but for atheistic reasons.

"It makes me feel uneasy going to a remodeled house, when I knew how it was before," Silvio explained.

Silvio boiled the pasta last, after everything else was made – the sauce with meatballs and sausages – as well as the fried veal cutlets.

The kids lit candles as Leah put on a Pavarotti CD. Silvio laid down plates full of food and sat at the head of the table. He then said grace – in Latin.

"*Benedic, Domine, nos et haec tua dona quae de Tua largeitate sumus sumpturi. Per Christum Dominum nostrum. Amen* (Bless us, O Lord, and these Thy gifts, which we are about to receive from Thy bounty. Through Christ our Lord)."

We all did the sign of the cross, except for Leah who was Jewish, and began to eat.

"This is what your great grandfather Patsy would call a "real 'Guinea' dinner," Silvio informed his children. We all look at Patsy's picture sitting on the living room mantle.

"Do you know why Italians and Sicilians were called Guineas?" I asked.

"Something to do with World War II," Silvio answered.

"It started long before that, when Italian and Sicilian immigrants landed in New York City at the turn of the twentieth century. The intended slur implies we are from the West African Coast. That we are non-white," I said.

"Kids, why don't you grab some soda from the refrigerator," Leah blurted out.

"In some cases it is kind of true though. We are not white people. Look how we tan? We don't golf. You ever wonder why you hang with black women, Kunta?"

Leah looked down at the floor, pretending not hear what Silvio had just said.

"Kids, are you okay in there?" Leah said, leaving the room.

After a cannoli, a few glasses of wine and the kids transported upstairs, Leah loosened up. She began talking about Silvio's "line of work."

"I'm proud of Silvio and his family. They are hard working, and like everybody in America, they hustle. I should know, I used to work for Bernie Madoff," Leah said sitting on the side patio while Silvio rolled a blunt. He lit it, puffed and passed it. Leah, puffed and passed to me.

"Did you have inkling that something wasn't kosher with Madoff while you working there?" I asked Leah.

"I did. We all did. I mean first Bernie had his own floor, that no one was allowed in. And that coincidently was where he kept all his records. I was a stock analyst, so I wouldn't really be purvey to them for any particular reason. But the way he kept it all so close to himself – on a floor no one was allowed to enter. We all thought, obviously he has something to hide."

She took a hit of weed and a sip of wine.

"The most remarkable thing that will always stick out in my mind," Leah added, "Is how normal it all seemed. We were insulated from the harsh, evil reality that Madoff truly was – with his plush, corporate headquarters, designed to convey infallibility,"

When the blunt was spent, we went inside. Silvio had made his order list of who got what, and we went down to the basement.

Downstairs were two card tables and a pile of what looked like green footballs and what I first thought was a fax machine. It turned out to be vacuum sealer.

"Each one of these is a exactly a pound. Now we need to break them up, weigh and repackage them into zips (ounces) and QP's," Silvio said.

It was a long night and we had only broken up twenty pounds. Fifty of the one hundred pounds – which was back at the studio – was going straight to Uncle Frank on the Upper West Side. Silvio held back ten for Monday's delivery and stashed another twenty back at the studio for his delivery service. That weight would be broken down by his cousins into zips and grams – who would then deliver it throughout downtown Manhattan.

The next morning Silvio and I hopped in his black, 2009 Maserati GranTurismo. It was an Italian Batmobile.

2009 Maserati GranTurismo

Tieless, Silvio wore a dark gray Ralph Lauren Wool Nigel Jacket and scarf from the "black label." He looked more like a flower shop manager than a drug dealer with twenty pounds of weed, bagged separately into QP's and zips. Of course, that was the whole point.

The first stop was the U.S. Post Office in Scarsdale where Silvio overnighted packages to Phoenix, Green Bay and Charlotte.

Why Scarsdale?

"It's the last place in America anyone would think weed is being overnighted," Silvio said. "But I switch it up all the time."

He had many clients in professional sports – football, basketball and hockey (none in baseball) and several well known rappers too. Today he had planned to visit folks and sample his new bud.

We walked across Scarsdale from the post office, cut through the colossal faux Tudor, Harwood Building built in 1928. Inside the main hall it was like a castle from the middle ages. We wound through another Tudor building that had no doors and then made a left to Zachy's Wine and Liquor.

There, Silvio loaded up on expensive vintage wine and liquor for customers. Afterwards, he hit Lange's Deli for few chicken cutlets on a roll, chips and a soda.

The first customer lived in Scarsdale, or at least he had a house there. Someone so famous, that even if I just mentioned his profession, it would be easy to figure out who he was. His wife is equally up there in the celebrity universe. We made a left into the driveway and drove up to the front door. Some flack walked out with an black envelope filled with cash. Silvio handed her a bag with two bottles of red wine and two vacuumed sealed QP's wrapped in gold paper. The couple observed from the bedroom window on the second floor. We both looked up at them. She waved at us and Silvio waved back and quickly sped off back down the driveway.

Alpine, New Jersey was next. Silvio made several stops at mansions so opulent, I thought Donald Trump just might walk out the front door of one of them.

We then drove to Dix Hill in Long Island, New York, where Silvio made a few more stops to the tri-state area's rich and famous. Then to Sea Cliff. Silvio sold so many zips there I lost track of what he unloaded.

Sometimes there was an intermediary, other times the client walked out himself. Silvio seemed to enjoy talking to famous people, and was able to overlap the social and business aspects of his profession with ease.

We drove back to city to settle up with Uncle Frank. We first stopped by the studio, where Silvio changed into what he called his "(John) Gotti suit." It was a Brioni, a custom tailored, silk, dark gray, metallic suit. It made Silvio look both stupid and menacing.

"I only wear this fucking thing when I meet with Frankie" Silvio informed me, slightly embarrassed by the ol'- school-mobster-tough-guy-suit.

When we got to the Upper West Side, Frank put in another fifty pound order for the following Monday.

"I don't know where you get it, but this shit is moving fast Sil," Frank told his nephew.

"Fresh California bud, that's all it is."

"And how much do you make off my back?" Frank asked.

"Yo," Silvio shot back, "Nobody has a better deal in Manhattan than you, and nobody knows that better than you … Frankie."

"Just remember your place Sil," Uncle Frank said. "Don't forget who is in charge here."

"Yeah sure, Frankie," Silvio shot back with a hint of "whatever."

"You better watch your fucking tone with me, nephew," Uncle Frank said in a blunt, threating manner. "Punks like you can't remember last week, you have no concept of seniority, of respect for the people who came before you. You see, I was the one who paved these streets you walk on today. I was the one who fought and bled on these streets while you sat in your gold plated crib in Fort Lee and Scarsdale. Everything you got was given to you, handed to you like a fucking Kennedy. But you are just a stupid, spoiled little nothing who got lucky. I know what you're up to nephew, you look at everything I have pulled together here over decades like a landing pad for your future. I got news for you, I'll be here a lot longer than you will ever be. I've been through hell and back, you never even made it out of Westchester," Frank bellowed to Silvio.

Silvio stayed silent, but you could see his eyes were saying "keep barking old dog. You don't think I notice that the louder you get with age … it's a sign of weakness?"

Frank looked at Silvio with an ice grill stare, just hoping Silvio would crack and take a swing at him, sparking a fight.

Silvio didn't take the bait. He put his hand out.

Frank walked in closer, eyes bulging with rage. He slapped the brick of hundred dollar bills into Silvio's hand.

Case closed. Silvio made his point without saying a word and walked off.

"See you next week Frankie," Silvio said on the way out.

Uncle Frank's eyes followed Silvio until he reached the door. He went to the window and watched his nephew click the remote on his new whip and hop in.

"You still here fish boy?" Frank said to me.

By the time he turned back around I was already gone.

We drove back to the Lower East Side, where Silvio checked in on his cousins counting cash after closing up for the night. The five of them pulled in about fifteen grand each – a good night.

Silvio called his little brother Luigi and asked him to meet him at his favorite restaurant in Manhattan, Pete's Tavern, the oldest con-tinuously operating restaurant in New York. Sacred ground for Silvio. No whores, busi-ness partners or music pals ever broke bread with Silvio there. It was where Silvio would take his mother on Mother's day and his daughters on their birthday.

The "O Henry Booth" at Pete's Tavern, New York City.

"*Solo mia famiglia,*" Silvio told me in the cab on the way to 18th Street near Union Square. "Only my family."

Not sure of what he was implying, I thought maybe Silvio would pull the cab over and drop me off before we got to the place. Instead he handed me some red, high-dosed cannabis candy he got from the Pink Hand.

"I want to flood the market with these soon, tell me what you think," Silvio said.

I opened one and ate it. I was about to open the rest when, Silvio stepped in.

"Whoa, slow down Kunta," Silvio said. "One dose is enough."

Silvio popped a few himself.

"For a first timer," Silvio added.

I proceeded to open and eat the rest.

The cab let us off outside our stop, and we walked under the black awning into the old red brick building. Silvio requested a wood booth, as he always did. But it was already waiting for him thanks to Luigi actually showing up on time.

"You get later and later with age," Luigi said, while he put his arms around Silvio and embraced his older brother.

"I've been hanging around Bobby De Niro too much lately," Silvio joked.

"Hey, It's Bobby Kunta-Kinte De Niro here," Luigi said, in a loud mocking New York Italian accent. I was not sure if he was mocking me or his older brother, but it certainly took the air out of the place when everybody looked at us.

Luigi had just broken Silvio's most important rule; never draw attention to yourself in public.

I hadn't seen Luigi in probably decades, but it was like not a day had gone by. We all sat down in the "O. Henry" booth. Luigi had already ordered wine, a pitcher of Pete's homebrewed beer, a plate of cold anti-pasta and two plates of fried calamari. Silvio sat under a framed news clipping of Abraham Lincoln.

Silvio ordered several plates of Spaghetti Arrabbiata, Spaghetti with Veal Meatballs and Chopped Mesclun Salad with Chicken. He then ordered three grilled 16oz New York Sirloin Steaks, three Half Spring Chickens, three jumbo burgers and a few orders of steak fries. Then he asked for some plates of prime rib and fried scallops too.

"Jesus Christ, Sil," Luigi said. " You got enough food to feed the Israeli Army."

"We are going to need it," Silvio said, pouring himself a beer.

"Let me guess, Uncle Frank again?" Luigi asked.

"Lou, I've had it with the crazy Viet Nam vet rants, he gives me."

"What are you going to do? He's Bob Barker, he runs the whole show. The king of the Eboli family from New York all the way down the coastline. There isn't a bagel made in Florida that Frankie doesn't get a nickel from," Luigi said.

"I thought it was a penny," Silvio said.

"You are going to just have to wait till the old fuck is dead, before you don't have deal with him anymore. And I'm willing to bet that won't be long from now. You're not the only one he rakes over the coals, Sil, and somebody in the family will step in, do the right thing when you least expect it," Luigi said.

"Why can't I just do the right thing?" Silvio said

"Because you are not that fucking insane, you are going to have to just chill," Luigi said. "The days of Tommy and Patsy riding up West 17 to Swan Lake are over, Rambo. Cell phones, security cameras at gas stations and traffic lights. You're traced everywhere you go."

"I don't really want to kill Frankie, I just want to push him out. Give him an early retirement," Silvio said.

"Retirement?" Luigi said. "Frankie will never retire, even if he was hit by a bus and was crippled from the neck down. Even if he was just a head in a jar, he would still hang on to power, gurgling on IV solution."

"I don't get it. He is deep into his 60's. He has tons of money ..."

"It's not about the money, it's about power and how he perceives himself, and more importantly how he thinks others perceive him. That is what he cares about most," Luigi said.

"That's precisely why Uncle Frank is so irate. You treated him like a old fart in a sweat suit, schlepping around track with a flask and an old egg sandwich," I said.

"He is buying bud from me," Silvio said. "I don't work for him."

"That's the rub brother. He thinks you do work for him. That's why he wants his price so low. He thinks he is entitled to it because of seniority," Luigi said. "In Frank's mind, he should be making off of you, not the other way around."

"I don't give a fuck. The money I make, is not worth the stress."

The food started to arrive and attention shifted to the table. Silvio realized he was stuck with Uncle Frank, but all he wanted to do was eat. He was stoned out of his mind, and just wanted to forget it all for a while.

The next morning, Silvio showed me how he sold weed online through "The Onion Router." TOR is a free software that enables users total "anonymity." Silvio used Bitcoin for online payment. When orders would come in online and payment was received, one of Silvio's cousins would run to the post office and ship a package out.

Silvio was a staple in New York's Hip-Hop community, and had many clients working in the industry. He sold to everybody, from the Wu Tang Clan to record label accountants. He sold to artists, actors and musicians of all ages and genres.

Wu Tang Clan

One night we went to a private party thrown by a big label for a well known Grammy winning R & B singer's new CD release. When Silvio walked in he was wearing $500 vintage ripped Levi Jeans, a white t-shirt and a black loose fitting John Varvatos sports coat. He also wore super high end accessories, diamond cufflinks and a canary diamond encrusted watch, both from Asprey. He walked around the room, shaking hands and handing out free cannabis candy to everybody he could. At the bar, he was surrounded by celebrities of all levels of fame, looking to score bud in the future. Less than an hour later, Silvio asked me to hold his "ice" while he went downstairs and had a threesome with two models in the night club wine cellar.

Early the next morning, Silvio texted me.

Get ready. Going to Poughkeepsie.

There was something jarring about Silvio's text, so early in the morning. I called my girlfriend.

"I think Silvio is going to kill me," I told her.

"Why do you think that?"

"I don't know. I got this weird feeling. I keep waiting for the moment when Silvio gets high, and his paranoia will kick in and start to rethink giving me total access to his criminal operation."

"Do you know how many times you have said this to me since you took this assignment?" my girlfriend asked.

"I know once or twice before."

"Try five times in like in six weeks."

"But this is it. He says we are going to Poughkeepsie. That's a little strange don't you think?" I ask.

"You know, to be honest, you seem like the one who's paranoid here, not Silvio. From what I see and hear, he is as calm as a clam. Your the one whose losing their shit."

She was right. Maybe it was all too overwhelming for me. Silvio's whole lifestyle was way beyond my realm of experience. It felt like a runaway train. Maybe, Silvio really wanted to get caught, and that his nightly ritual of reckless behavior in clubs was a loud cry for help. That he too, like myself wanted a break from his life.

We drove up north on the New York State Thruway in a black, 2006 Mercedes Benz CLS 55 AMG. He brought along some "muscle" – two scary looking dudes who looked like they were born and raised in an Albanian gulag. I really thought this was my final night the longer we drove upstate. Yet I was in the back seat, I still had my cell phone and the door was unlocked. I started to realize how right my girl really was.

Silvio had planned to meet Fat Johnny, Poughkeepsie's main bud distributor at Mahoney's, a large Irish bar by the train station.

"You guys wait here," Silvio said to his goons.

He looked at me.

"You, follow me."

The joint was eerily empty, with flat screens all playing different sporting events. We walked in, passed a stairwell to the second floor and heard a piano, old honky-tonk from the Wild West. It was Fat Johnny's I-Phone. He turned around when he saw us and grabbed his drink.

"Howdy," Silvio said.

"Clint Eastwood, does whatever the fuck he wants, haven't seen you in a while," Fat Johnny said.

Silvio looked puzzled at the reference, but went to the bar and ordered a pitcher of beer and a round of whiskey.

Johnny walked over to Silvio.

"Who the fuck is your friend?"

"He's cool," Silvio said back calmly.

"That's not what I heard," Johnny shot back. "I heard he is a fucking journalist or some shit."

"He is my biographer."

"What did you say? I didn't hear that," Johnny said.

Silvio paused.

"My biographer."

Fat Johnny burst out laughing.

"Oh that's just great. And when exactly were you planning on me telling this exciting news?" Johnny asked sarcastically.

Silvio was speechless.

"This is a serious breech of trust," Johnny said.

"No it's not," Silvio shot back. "He is with me. It's cool. If it wasn't he wouldn't be here."

"This meeting is over. Call me when you shake off the paparazzi," he downed his shot, got up and walked out.

Silvio didn't say a word. I followed his lead. But I kept wondering to myself, as Silvio ordered two more doubles of whiskey.

Who told Fat Johnny I was a journalist?

Then, Silvio's muscle burst in, late. Silvio looked at them like the morons they were.

I was waiting for Silvio to say something on the car ride home, but he said nothing. He looked out the window the entire time. I could tell his wheels were spinning upstairs. His demeanor was calm, as if he had worked out who double-crossed him with Fat Johnny.

We got back to city by late afternoon. Silvio had to check in on another project.

Silvio provided under-the-table construction deals for business owners who could not otherwise afford it. On the Lower East Side, the owner of a Chinese dumpling house wanted to expand beyond their small kitchen. "Dumpling," as the heavy set Chinaman was called around the neighborhood, managed to buy an old bar that had gone out of business, but was short of funds to remodel the place legally with city permits and union labor.

He turned to Silvio a few weeks ago, after asking other immigrant merchants for advice around the neighborhood about what to do. After a sizable cash advance, Silvio sent his crew to work on the interior. Dumpling would pay the crew cash … daily. Dumpling was not able to keep up with what he owed, so Silvio's crew shifted into slowdown mode.

When we got there Silvio's guys were drinking. He turned to his site manager Joey and asked him what was going on.

"I don't know man, I'm just wandering around," Joey said half drunk.

"Go get Dumpling," Silvio ordered.

Joey walked off and brought Dumpling back with him. Dumpling was as nervous as Silvio was agitated. Silvio didn't waste time with any preamble.

"What the fuck is going on here?"

Dumpling looked at the muscle at Silvio's side.

"I'm very sorry … but I have no more money. I have given you everything I have, and nothing is complete. I have no more to give."

Silvio looked like he was about to smash in Dumpling's face. Then, he looked at me taking notes at the bar. He took a deep breath and shifted gears.

"Can you at least feed my workers? I want twenty dozen dumplings, now," Silvio ordered.

"Yes, yes. Right away," Dumpling said, backing up as quickly as possible.

"Dumpling," Silvio yelled, "half of those are for me."

"Yes," Dumpling said as he opened the back door and ran down the block as fast as he could.

"And some fried fucking rice," Silvio said from outside the door.

When Dumpling got back, he put two large bags on the bar.

Silvio thanked him. Dumpling looked at Silvio waiting for the other shoe to drop.

Silvio smiled.

"We'll work something out Dumpling," Silvio said disarming the tension in the air. Dumpling looked pleased just to be walking out without any broken bones and all his fingers. He bowed to Silvio and started moving to the exit. Silvio looked forward, ignoring Dumpling's movements.

After Dumpling ran off, Silvio paid his crew out of his own pocket and ordered them a dozen pizzas with the works. He then told them to "destroy everything" in the place and "paint the joint in dumplings" and rice afterwards.

Silvio demonstrated. He took a hammer and smashed a floor tile, took the tiles and threw them at the wall length mirror behind the bar, shattering it down the middle vertically. He went over to the corner of the bar by the door where Dumpling left the food, pulled out a box of dumplings and a box of rice from one of the bags walked back to the center bar and hurled the dumplings as hard as he could at the wall, splashing dumpling sauce and rice all over. He then walked over to the other corner of the bar and picked up a long heavy rusty spike lying on the floor. He picked it up, climbed on top the of the bar and walked to the center of it. He lifted the spike over his head and jammed it into the bar top several times. He jumped down and grabbed a hand held power saw, plugged it in to the wall and turned it on. He walked to the end of the bar where he got the spike and ran the buzzing saw down the top of the bar, scattering wood chips into the air. He then picked up a sledge hammer and plowed it through a plaster wall. He did it over and over, poking holes with each whack.

Silvio turned around slightly winded and looked at his crew.

"That how I want it," Silvio said.

The crew of about five plus the muscle put on their hard hats and protective eyewear and proceeded to rip the place apart. I couldn't believe what I was witnessing. The chaos, the mayhem, the grinding sounds of metal, wood and cement. Pieces of tile flew in all directions. Silvio walked over to me, his eyes were dead.

"I live for shit like this," Silvio said. He handed me a few hundred dollar bills and told me to wait for the pizza. He pulled out another box of dumplings from the take out bag and set it down on the bar. He opened the box and ate a dumpling.

"Great fucking dumplings," he said and walked off to continue demolishing the inside section of the bar.

I picked up a dumpling myself. He was right. They were great dumplings.

I heard a knock at the door and opened it. It was the pizza driver. His jaw dropped as he looked at eight grown men going to town on the joint.

He walked over to the bar with the pizzas and saw the dumplings, which confused him even more. He set the pizzas down on the bar. I handed him the money which included a huge tip. He looked at me overjoyed and ran out of the place.

As we exited the bar, Silvio made reservations for two rooms at the St. Regis Hotel. In the car, he called his favorite escort service in Manhattan and ordered up a slew of girls for the night. He rolled a blunt and lit it up. We drove uptown to what Silvio called a "French joint," named Daniel. His muscle dropped us off and parked the Benz back at the Regis.

The girls soon walked in and sat down with us. Silvio ordered so much food it was a blur. There was champagne and caviar on every horizontal surface before dinner arrived.

Silvio looked at me.

"Not a bad day," Silvio said, "other then losing a hundred grand up state."

Silvio and the girls hailed a cab and got to the Regis a stumbling mess. He handed me a room key and we parted ways. When I opened the door there were three girls watching TV and eating room service, waiting for my arrival.

Despite all the seductive trappings for someone in his line of business – the drugs, the girls, the clubs, the celebrity friends – Silvio craved for one thing above all else.

Routine.

In the morning Silvio bought coffee and Nat Shermans at Grand Central. At Astor Place we would walk down Saint Marks Street towards the studio. Inside, we would light up and Silvio would send me out more coffee and a bacon-egg-and-cheese on a roll from the Mexican joint on the corner. He worked in the studio until 2PM, breaking for burgers and pierogis at Veselka.

At 3PM, Silvio hustled. The phone would ring nonstop. He might have ten messages waiting for him after talking to one client for less than a minute.

Silvio had a Vespa, but for large orders, he just hopped in a cab.

Wrapping up around 7PM, Silvio would head back to the studio. He would send me out for Amstels and kinishs before he would count his money with his drivers, roll another one, then we bounce to dinner. We would then hit Katz's Delicatessen, Lombardi's, or sometimes Peter Luger's in Brooklyn to meet with friends or family.

Katz's Deli, Lower East Side, New York City.

At night we would hit VIP parties, B-list star rooftop barbecues, or nightclubs where we would drink $55 martinis. Silvio also knew where in Manhattan to pick up the hottest girls and the best late night burgers in one shot – The Burger Joint, practically hidden in the lobby of the Le Parker Meridien Hotel.

The Burger Joint, Le Parker Meridien Hotel, New York

In November, we watched the Yankees win the final game of the World Series at the 40/40 Club, Jay Z's sports bar on 25th Street. When the party eventually spilled out into the street, we partied some more at McSorley's Ale House. From there we wandered into a diner for a few orders of waffles and fried chicken.

When the sun rose, we walked to the studio. Silvio sent me to get coffee around the corner.

On my way back I looked down and saw a small trail of bud on the sidewalk. I followed it back to Silvio's studio door. I looked down and saw Silvio sprawled out on the floor, blood pouring from his head, his hair and face caked in bud.

"Get Afan," Silvio calmly said.

Afan, Silvio's muscle – a Croatian veteran of the Bosnian War with missing finger tips – lived next door. I ran and knocked.

Silvio's Studio door, Lower East Side, New York,

Afan opened his door, barefoot, wearing red and white-striped pajamas. He grabbed his keys and leather overcoat, woke up his girlfriend and double parked his van outside the studio entrance. While we got Silvio in the van, Afan's old lady swept the bud off the stoop.

"Get me to White Plains Hospital!" Silvio said, "Get me out of the city."

"Kunta, you're not safe either," Silvio said to me.

Afan dropped me off at Grand Central, with an address of a "friend" of Silvio with an empty furnished apartment near Columbus Circle. I called my girl, Orleans and told her grab our pit-bull and cab it uptown.

"What's going on?" Orleans asked.

That evening, we found a small cabin for rent near Swan Lake – in the Catskills – hidden in the woods behind a farm. The place had an outdoor shower, a wood stove and was totally off the grid.

The next day, Afan dropped by with Silvio's stash from the studio. He handed me some money, a QP and a few grams of hash, a "gift" he said "from

On the the lam: Cabin Toby Rogers hid out in, Swan Lake, New York.

Silvio." We then drove – along with my girl and dog – to Swan Lake.

Along the way, Afan told me what went down the day before.

When I went for coffee, a friend of an old customer walked into the studio and wanted to buy some weed. Silvio was pissed that he just rolled in like that. When Silvio turned around, he got sucker-punched in the back of the head.

Silvio hit the floor, thinking an amplifier from above fell on him before he briefly blacked out, The attacker knew right where to go, grabbed a large bag of Diesel from a drum case and dashed back towards the entrance.

As he ran up the steps Silvio grabbed the bottom right corner of the bag and tore a hole, causing bud to rain on his head. The robber then kicked Silvio in the chest and down the steps. His head hit the top the door frame, and blood began to run out of his head in small streams when he hit the floor.

Silvio believed that the hit might have been orchestrated – after all these years – by his old boss, Chief.

It took a few days to acclimate from the noisy streets of Lower East Side and Columbus Circle to chopping wood deep in the quiet, snowy woods of the Catskills. But after all that had gone down, it was a much needed change of pace.

Still recovering from the attack, I called Silvio. He had taken his family to a large remote villa on the Island of Tobago with a private bay … "for the holidays."

"Your kidding, Swan Lake?" Silvio asked.

"Why do you say that?"

"Tommy and Patsy dumped a lot bodies in Swan Lake back in the day. I'd say at least twenty."

"That's a strange coincidence," I said.

Silvio did not think so.

"Do me a favor Kunta? Don't call me for a while."

When Silvio got back from the Caribbean after the New Year, he laid low, really low. He closed up his music studio on the Lower

Swan Lake, Swan Lake, New York.

East Side and moved the equipment to a small storage house in New Canaan, Connecticut

Within a week on the lam in Swan Lake, my girlfriend got pregnant. We stayed the winter in Swan Lake, then later moved north, into the Adirondacks.

I called Silvio to ask if it was safe to live a normal life again.

"I don't fucking know," Silvio said. "What do you want, a fucking notarized letter?"

That wasn't exactly the answer I was looking for.

"I'm sorry bout this Kunta, we are both in the same boat. As soon as we take care of it, I'll be in touch. You just keep writing" Silvio said.

You just keep writing.

That last sentence echoed in my mind for some time. As if his story was all that mattered.

After that phone call, I wasn't sure if I would be on the lam for another five weeks … or five years.

At least, Silvio covered all the expenses hopscotching around, but it felt like indentured servitude. After Swan Lake, we moved to Prattsville, Troy, Watervliet, Blue Mountain Lake, Skaneateles, Lake Luzerne, and finally Catskill. In Catskill we lived in an old abandoned train station behind the Catskill River that had been converted into a house. My daughter was born while we were in Blue Mountain Lake.

Toby Rogers and his daughter at Skaneateles Lake, Skaneateles, New York.

At Blue Mountain Lake we lived at a resort, that we believed was as remote as you can get. But within a few weeks of moving there, a large band of Afghanis rented the house behind us. My pastoral sensibilities about the Silk Road region did not stop me from thinking something was seriously wrong with dozens of Afghani's floating around all weekend. Some drank, some smoked weed, others prayed in the direction of Mecca, and they all gambled – young and old. One of the group, Ahmed Zia, told me was a "halal" butcher and to call him when I got back to the city if I ever wanted "hand-slaughtered" meat.

My suspicions turned out to be valid, it seems, later, when I got a knock on my door from a New York State Police Counter Terrorism Intelligence Unit Investigator and Stephen D. of the United States Border Patrol (and the Central Intelligence Agency).

They asked me the standard questions, did the Afghani's pray to Mecca, performed any "cleansing rituals," or had they expressed any hatred toward the Untied States. They asked me what I had been asking myself since the Afghanis had left.

"What was a bunch of Afghani's doing way up here in the Adirondacks the middle of nowhere?" Stephen asked me.

As they were getting ready to leave, Stephen walked back over to me from his SUV.

"I just have one more thing, was this guy here?"

Stephen, opened a folder with a mug shot and other info.

"Oh yeah, he was here for sure, but he has a beard now."

Stephen looked like I just told him the worst news ever. He got quiet for moment, absorbing what I said, regained his composure

"OK. Thank you," Stephen said and drove off.

I called Silvio and told him what went down.

"What the fuck?" Silvio roared.

As soon as my daughter was born, we moved to Skaneateles. Silvio kept us moving often to keep up us safe after the *Albany Times Union* announced my daughters birth.

We ended up Catskill, New York, in an old train station behind town on the Catskill River. I got a job as a reporter at the *Catskill Daily Mail*.

Catskill is a town in almost total dilapidation, and its local

Old Train Station, Catskill, New York.

paper reflects the community they cover. The *Daily Mail*, *Hudson Register-Star*, *Chatham Courier*, *Windham Journal*, *The Mountain Eagle*, *The Ravena News-Herald*, and *Greene County News* – all owned by Johnson Newspapers in Watertown, New York – The office was the perfect storm of everything that can go wrong at a local paper.

Editors terrified of a dysfunctional management, reporters running on empty and totally uninterested in what they write about, overprinting papers to inflate circulation numbers and overcharge advertisers, picking sides in elections, a publisher more interested in watching porn and an "Executive Editor" – who everybody in the office hated – all added up to an unmitigated disaster.

My editors operated like the characters in *The Twilight Zone* who trembled all day under their fake smiles saying and doing anything to please the little supernatural child who made his family celebrate his birthday everyday.

The senior reporter – a cross between Pete Seeger and Charles Manson – was the only reporter that lasted more then six months.

He would roam the halls and babble to himself while nuking a Mexican TV dinner in the microwave. He'd then walk into the newsroom, holding the hot tray of enchiladas and announced to the newsroom as profoundly as he could, "the 60's never existed, man. It never happened."

He'd then sat down at his desk, and continued to elaborate on his brilliant proclamation while chunks of beef enchilada and brown sauce dribbled down his white, "duck-dynasty" beard.

After a few months I began realize what it must be like to work for a paper in North Korea, where up is down and two plus two equals five.

I soon accepted another job at the *Berkshire Record* in Western Massachusetts, mainly because they didn't have a website at the time.

But that was like jumping from the frying pan into the fire.

We moved to Stockbridge, Massachusetts, and lived in an old farm house off the grid with nothing in our names. It was owned by "classical music mystery" novelist Gerald Elias, whose books are so bad that reading one paragraph of the latest novel gave me writer's block for a week.

I had been hired over the phone, so my first day on the job at the *Record* was my first time at the office and meeting staff.

The first thing I saw when I walked in was a large painting of circus clowns on the wall. This served as the perfect analogy of the place. It also smelled, that dry-skin retirement-home smell. As I walked around the "office" which was an old, dust-covered, spooky house in Great Barrington, I truly felt I was living in the opening scenes of a Tim Burton film.

I looked up the stairway, as dust floated by above me, and then a head appeared over the stairwell at the top floor. She looked like Crypt Keeper from *Tales of the Crypt*.

"You," the publisher's wife Donna bellowed down the stairway. "Are you Toby?"

"Yes."

"Come here," Donna requested and schlepped out of my view.

I walked up the creaking stairway and smelled old bananas and burnt coffee along the way.

As soon as we stopped shaking hands, Donna starting name dropping, "You will love it here darling, Victor George's daughter works downstairs," she said as she got real close, starting playing with my hair in her hand like I was her new toy. Was it the spice I just smoked in the parking lot or did she try to kiss me?

Things went down hill as soon as I met Donna's husband Anthony, and their disturbed son Alexis. Almost everyday, they would yell at staff or each other. One day Alexis ran into the newsroom crying.

"Mom, Shut up!" Alexis yelled, tears rolled down his face as he stomped his shoes and held his ears shut.

The *Record*'s "news editor," spent his time writing pithy features on fire engine companies that belonged to fictitious Berkshire towns and other silly adventures no one read. He spoke with a fake British accent, and would sing Broadway show tunes at full volume. The rest of the staff would roll their eyes and laugh to themselves all day.

Every morning, Anthony would walk into the newsroom and assign one of us a story he had read in the daily *Berkshire Eagle*. That was the level of his newspaper ingenuity. He looked like Senator Chris Dodd's twin and acted like him too. When he spoke to someone his eyes and face would dart all around, almost afraid to ever give anyone eye contact.

He walked over to my desk the first day and assigned me an expose on sandwich boards in Lenox.

"Now Toby, this sandwich board story, its radioactive. Emotions run high on both sides of the sandwich board debate, and the things you write, could spark an reaction we would never anticipate. So I want you to be as fair and diplomatic to both sides, just like I read in this morning's *Eagle*.

For the next seven hours, Anthony would call me, walk over to my desk or just yell from upstairs every 20 minutes.

"Toby. Sandwich boards. Where's the story?"

Just to mess with his head, I waited until the last minute to hand it in. He calls got more frequent and panic stricken.

"Toby! Sandwich boards! I got to have the sandwich boards' story now! It just too delicate and an important story to just throw in at the last minute. So I got to see the sandwich board story now, no more excuses and delays. Sandwich boards. You got to give me the sandwich boards' piece," Anthony repeated over and over.

It all got old fast. I quickly moved on and began freelancing with the *Berkshire Eagle*.

I also started freelancing for *High Times* again. My favorite writer there, Chris Simunek had became Editor-In-Chief. He had been a cultivation editor when I first met him in 1998, and was one of most gifted feature writers alive.

Simunek was just getting his groove as boss when we first spoke after seven years. With his new onslaught of responsibilities, my work, including a 6000 word feature I

HIGH TIMES magazine, 40-years old and still growing after all these years.

had developed on Silvio appeared to be slipping through the cracks. Hurricane Sandy didn't help either. Then *High Times* moved from Park Ave to 57th Street in Manhattan.

The timing just seemed off between us.

In the spring of 2013, Silvio emailed me, asking me to call.

"Yeah, Kunta, you're safe. Its all over. I got a studio in Dumbo, Brooklyn, set for you and the family. It's an awesome, upscale neighborhood, right by Grimaldi's," Silvio told me, "It's like the Upper East Side of Brooklyn."

Grimaldi's, Dumbo, Brooklyn , New York.

"What do you mean by safe?" I asked.

"The guy is in a mental ward," Silvio informed me and hung up.

It had been almost four years since I left Manhattan in 2009. The city felt different, or was it me who changed after living in some of the remote areas of New York? Our last destination on the lam was a

80-acre ranch in Canaan, New York. It was so remote and quiet that all you'd hear were trees rustling and the refrigerator hum.

We met at Peter Luger's in Williamsburg. We looked like we had just came out of the woods.

"You guys smell like burnt wood," Silvio said.

"Well, if you had to run a wood stove 24/7 for five months, you would too," I said back.

Silvio ordered "Steak for Three" from the "aging box," and a few "double-thick Lamb Chops" and several orders of fries.

"Welcome back, brother," Silvio said as graciously as possible.

We all toasted our return to the Big Apple with oversized drinks.

It was surreal acclimating to an area I had grown up in. But that was how long I had been away. For four years I looked over my shoulder and sat in the corner booth facing the door at restaurants. I didn't realize how crazy being on the lam was until I did not have to do it anymore.

It was all over, and I was finally home.

The apartment was small, but my family and I walked around, Dumbo free from fear. We ate at outdoor cafes and saw live music, not having to worry that someone might be out there lurking, waiting for the right time to strike.

A few weeks later, I get text from Silvio early in the morning.

Union Square. Gandhi statue. Noon Sharp. Wear a suit.

Why? I ask.

No response.

Notebook? I ask.

No showbiz today. This is work. Silvio replied

Silvio debriefed me in Union Square, sitting under the Mahatma.

He had starting seeing a young Colombian model in the fall of 2011. They met at the Occupy Wall Street Protest site, Zuccotti Park, after Silvio watched the protests on television, got wasted

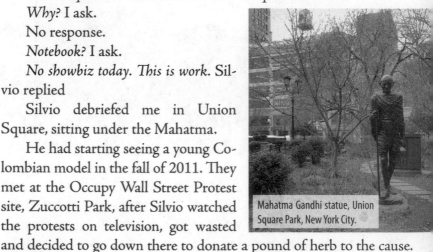

Mahatma Gandhi statue, Union Square Park, New York City.

and decided to go down there to donate a pound of herb to the cause.

Her name was Rosita and her father, Carlos, was an old coke kingpin who was now running crystal meth into the U.S. from Bogota airport from a 800 acre "horse farm" in the countryside. Rosita was on her way to becoming a well known fashion model until her career derailed over crack. When Silvio got her clean, her family treated him like royalty.

"How did she get addicted to crack?" I ask.

"She smoked it," Silvio answered.

"A few months ago, another cocaine princess that Rosy knew was smoking crack in front of her daughter. Rosy called CPS and now this bitch's family has offered Rosy $250,000 to recant her statement."

"Sil! That's fucking extortion! You go to jail for that."

"No it's not. They called and made the fucking offer to us," Silvio said, "Rosy asked me for protection."

"Why did you call me?" I ask.

"For protection," Silvio said.

"Are fucking you insane!" I said, "Where's Afan?"

"I had to get rid of him, don't ask why."

"So you want *me* to kill somebody?"

"Fuck no. Just look as scary as possible," Silvio said.

Then a limousine pulled up. The driver got out and walked over to us, holding a small sports bag. He walked over and handed me the bag.

"Sir. I believe you left this in the car this morning," the driver said.

I say nothing and give the most menacing glare I can.

The driver doesn't miss a beat, tips his hat and bows slightly before leaving.

"Good day, Sir," the driver says before opening the car door stepping in and driving off.

"See how easy that was?" Silvio said.

" I should just walk," I tell Silvio.

"I wouldn't do that," a thick South American female voice from behind me said.

I turned around and saw a gorgeous mocha skinned woman with long black hair, tight jeans and tons of swag walking towards me.

It was Rosita.

"Then I'd have to hurt you," Rosita said with a seductive smile.

We get back to Silvio's studio and Rosita cuts the cash.

"How much does your 'bodyguard' get?" Rosita asked sarcastically.

"Ten," Sivio said.

Rosita threw me small backpack and walked over holding $50,000 in her hands.

"Nobody respects writers anymore, do they?" Rosita said real close up to me.

"All in a days work," Sivio said walking over. Rosita grabs a bottle of Cristal from the fridge. She pops it open, takes a swig and passes it off. She then lights a blunt, takes two hits and hands it to me.

I hopped in a cab to Grand Central Station and bought a round trip to Scarsdale. I walked from the Scarsdale station up Garth Road. The old movie house was torn down, and the old fish shop was now a cell phone store. I walked across the street into the woods and towards the Bronx River. There, stood an old oak tree with a hole under a root. I stuffed the money – now wrapped in several dark green garbage bags in the hole and filled it over with dirt and rocks. I put a razor blade inside the pile and sealed it up with sticks and leaves.

I trained back to Manhattan and met Silvio and Rosita at Masa, an infamous sushi house in Columbus Circle, with dinners starting at $450, $600 with Kobe beef. My girl and our daughter cabbed it over and rolled in late. Silvio ordered an

The Scarsdale Theater aka Scarsdale Plaza, Se tember 11, 1931 - July 4, 2002. Built as a homa to William Shakespeare's Globe Theater in Lond

other sushi plate and a plate of Kobe beef for my daughter.

It was eerily peaceful in the temple-like restaurant that evening. After dinner, we all waked around Central Park, Silvio and Rosita went their own way towards the old bandstand. My family and I went to the steps of the main fountain. I bought a hot pretzel and split it with my girl and daughter. A saxophone player in distance played, *Ruby My Dear*. My girl gave me smile I hadn't seen since we bolted to Swan Lake years ago

We got a cab back to Dumbo, Rosita and Silvio took one downtown.

A few hours later I get a text from Silvio.

Get over here ASAP.

I cab back to the Lower East Side. Run into the studio and there is Rosita crying and Silvio bleeding.

"What happened," I ask.

"We got robbed, all the cash from today is gone," Silvio informs me.

"All of it?" I ask.

"Both our cuts are gone," Silvio said.

"That's crazy. Who would even know you had it?" I ask.

"Things have changed since you left bro, no one had to know we had bricks of cash for this to happen," Silvio said.

I walk out and cab back to Dumbo. I pack the car and drive my family to Skaneateles Lake. I left the money stashed in Scarsdale. My girl and I didn't speak the entire ride upstate.

Other things had changed since we left New York City four years ago.

Weed was bubbling over onto the national landscape with voters in both Colorado and Washington passing referendums legalizing cannabis for recreational use.

In the summer of 2012, I began writing for a new American weed magazine called *Cannabis Now*. The magazine came out of nowhere in 2011 and starting popping up at Barnes & Noble right next to *High Times*.

I picked up a copy and emailed them a resume and some clippings.

A few weeks later I got a call from Jeremy, *Cannabis Now's* "Editor In Chief."

We spoke extensively about *Cannabis Now's* "mission."

Jeremy and the "publisher" Eugeno explained to me that *Cannabis Now* is an answer to what he described as *High Times'* "juvenile" attitude towards weed, that a "serious issue" that needs a "serious publication."

"Dispensaries don't want to carry *High Times* anymore than they want to sell *Cheech & Chong* DVDs. This industry wants to be taken seriously, and *High Times* does not reflect the 'times'. They are an embarrassment. That's why we are named *Cannabis Now*," Garcia said.

It was an unusual pitch, considering the only difference in content between both publications was that *Cannabis Now* had more boring, poorly-written articles and their layout was awful. It was like *Screw Magazine* claiming they are the "anti-*Playboy*."

In fact the only parallel between *High Times* and *Cannabis Now* was they were both magazines, and they both had pictures of weed.

Other than it was night and day.

Because of the inadvertent delays at *High Times*, I went and made one of the biggest mistakes of my career.

I sold the feature on the Ganja Godfather to *Cannabis Now*.

It didn't matter if *Cannabis Now* was offering double the money *High Times* was, it was a grave error on my part not to research a publication before putting my byline in it.

The feature received a positive response from *Cannabis Now's* small readership, and subsequently I was invited to work out of their Bozeman, Montana office.

The offer also came with free housing. Garcia told me that the "real" publisher Chris Fanuzzi "has a guest ranch" in Montana. Fanuzzi owned a successful weed dispensary called Lionheart in Bozeman.

Cannabis Now Magazine(CNM) appears to be a front for The Church of the Universal Triumphant (CUT), a cult based in Paradise Valley, Montana. It is owned by Chris Fanuzzi.

The living space I would be living in was pitched to me as a "resort" in Paradise Valley. " I grew up there," Fanuzzi told me.

What Fanuzzi did not tell me before I drove across the country from New York to Montana was that the Paradise Valley "resort," I and my family was headed toward in was in fact an old compound of a fanatical religious New Age cult called the Church Universal and Triumphant.

We rolled into Montana after driving through the Badlands of South Dakota and spent a night at the *Sacajawea Hotel* in Three

Forks, Montana. The next morning we drove to Bozeman and met Fanuzzi for breakfast. Instead of the laid back weed farmer I imagined on the phone, Fanuzzi was more Eminem circa-1999.

Fanuzzi started a strange awkward conversation about "family." He rambled on and on and made disconnected statements, which was unsettling after a three night day drive. My girl and my daughter went off to McDonalds to grab food while I ate with Fanuzzi. Fanuzzi drew me a map of the "resort" as well as directions to it.

We arrived in the afternoon. The "resort" was a total fucking wreck. A weird hippie and his old lady hobbled over from a warehouse they lived in. They looked like extras from a Woodstock reenactment and smelled of lentils, patchouli oil, cheep beer and menthols.

Their new age ramblings were hard to hear over the cars and RV-Campers constantly whizzing by on their way to Yellowstone Park. But the more I heard about "Planet X" and "alien slaves on Earth" the more creepier it all became.

Golden Ratio Ranch, also owned by Chris Fanuzzi, Emigrant Peak, Montana. The car in the driveway on the right belonged to Toby Rogers.

It was only after I arrived that I discovered that *Cannabis Now*, was just simply a front for a seriously vile, new age cult.

The Church Universal and Triumphant overlapped different religions together or "interfaced" them as they call it. Buddhism, Christianity and anything else they liked – including anti-semitic conspiracy theories, Tea Party and end of the world mumbo-jumbo.

Most in Paradise Valley hate CUT, and not just because they are all from New Jersey or California. Years ago members of CUT, including the Fanuzzi family, had their children taken away by the state. CUT's deep hatred of the government and perceived components of American life distanced themselves from the rest of Montana.

The "Golden Ratio Ranch" as its known, was repossessed by the bank, Big Sky Western, in 2007 and they let the place fall apart – unable to sell such a strange overdeveloped house. The weirdest part of the compound was the basement "spa."

One side of the "spa."

With Dr. Seuss like curved floors, walls and doors, the place got scarier with each step towards what I was told was a homemade enema machine. It was strapped to the ceiling and looked like a giant metallic spider with strange shower nozzles, darting from all directions under a message table.

"You should see the worms we pull out of people, this time around we are going to film it all and put it on Youtube," a Fanuzzi family member enthusiastically told me.

I was told by cult members that the Fanuzzi family believed that the property line of Golden Ratio perfectly paralleled the island of Manhattan, including its water currents.

The next day I woke up to total cacophony and the smell of bacon.

I walked into the kitchen and saw cult members and my girl yelling at each other. A bald ex-con looked the most heated. I ask him what's wrong.

"What's wrong? You have totally desecrated our temple, that's what's wrong," 'Gus' told me.

The entire compound reeked of bacon, but that was not all. They didn't tell me, but part of the "desecration" of the cult's compound was that my girlfriend was black and our daughter was mixed.

I started to realize how bad this was.

The downstairs we were supposed to live was infested with "desert mice" feces. Mixed with urine , it can be poisonous if it gets in into the lungs. The cleaning staff Fannuzi hired had to spray all the mice shit with bleach in order to kill the poison before attempting to clean it up.

So my racially-mixed family was forced to live in the main house of a white-supremacist-vegan cult after we cooked bacon in their rat-shit-infested "sacred temple." I wandered around the front of the compound and looked at the golden arches that stood over the front of the entrance way. I realized then how strange – almost alien like – and out of place they were from the rest of Montana and planet earth.

I called Silvio, who was in Columbia with Rosita.

"Where's your cut?" Silvio asks.

"Back in New York," I say, "I only took two grand with me."

"Your going to have to hold tight for few weeks until I get back," Silvio says.

The cult cut off my access to the Internet. I called Garcia at the *Cannabis Now* office in Berkley, California who played dumb and acted like he doesn't know what was going on.

A few days later Fanuzzi cut off the water.

That afternoon, something even more strange happened. Emigrant Peak caught on fire behind the compound.

The cult automatically blamed my two-year-old, racially-mixed daughter's presence in the compound for the wildfire.

The last night we were there, they held a "cleansing ceremony," which consisted of a white-people drum circle. They drummed about as well as they danced. Gus – a white man's white man – danced and played a didgeridoo and wore paint on his face. It was about as surreal a scene as you could imagine. A white supremacist cult mimicking a African griot to "cleanse" the compound of the presence of black people.

Meanwhile Silvio is having the time of his life in Columbia. He and Rosita were on a plush 800-acre horse ranch that her father owed. Because of Silvio's incredible good fortune – rescuing Rosita from crack addiction, Rosita's father, Carlos agrees to set Silvio up in the meth business in New York.

In the afternoons, Silvio and Carlos would walk along the beach front and discuss business arrangements. At night they would binge on Columbian BBQ and cocaine on the deck of an enormous Spanish villa.

Silvio flew home as we were drove back to New York from Montana.

After three days and nights on the road, I met up with Silvio at the Waverly Inn in the West Village. We ordered – my daughter had a $65 bowl of mac-n-cheese – and Silvio told me about his new business venture.

Waverly Inn, West Village, New York City.

Silvio and Rosita were going to run a high quality meth, nicknamed "Pepsi" on the street, through a Columbian embassy on the East Coast through diplomatic staff. Silvio would sell it exclusively to his Uncle Frank, who ran the upper West Side and planned to distribute it all over the tri-state area.

My girl had decided to take a few per-diem jobs upstate with contacts she had. In the early morning of September 10th, 2013 she died in a car accident in upstate New York.

I was about to call Silvio when I got a text from him.

McSorley's, now.

I text back and get no response. I call. Silvio picks up on the fourth ring.

"I need you to get over here, now."

"Orleans is dead," I tell Silvio.

"Get your daughter, get in a cab and meet me McSorley's," Silvio demands, *now!*

I walked through the old sawdust covered floor of the old 19th Century ale house, while I held my two year old daughter's left hand. Not much has changed in the bar since World War I. In a table in the back, I saw Silvio and Rosita sitting down at table under a painting of a chubby nude white woman. Both of their faces are dinged up bad.

"We got hit early this morning, again," Silvio explained. Silvio lost a huge pile of money, almost his entire first pay that was owed to Carlos.

You think the accident upstate–" I ask.

"I don't know yet. But I do know this," Silvio said

Through intelligence connections within the Columbian government, Rosita's family pinpointed that Silvio's Uncle Frank orchestrated the hit, only weeks after making the exchange with Silvio for the first time.

There was more.

Through email exchanges of various parties, it appeared that Uncle Frank had raped Silvio's younger sister Regina for years growing up. Silvio called and confronted Regina. She broke down, and confessed the whole epic nightmare to her older brother. Even when Regina was older she had been afraid to tell anyone, because she thought it would start a family war that would end in bloodbath.

"Ain't that some shit," Silvio said, barely able to contain himself, trembling in rage. "I knew this would happen, I saw it unfold in my mind flying down to Columbia. I wouldn't be surprised at all if Frankie had something to do with the accident," Silvio said.

"So what are we going to do?" I coldly ask.

"I'm way ahead of you Kunta," Silvio said. "That fat pedophile bastard Frankie eats almost every night at a restaurant called *Il Sorriso, Ristorante Italiano*, in Irvington, NY. When he is done stuffing his fat fucking face he walks down to the Hudson River and walks around a park until his train comes to take him back to Tudor City where he lives," Silvio explained.

The plan was to grab Frank in the park and stuff him in a small boat. A friend of Silvio had a boat at the Irvington Boat Club, next to the park. That boat would take us to a larger fishing boat that belonged to a contact with Fulton Market that will bring us all further out into the Atlantic Ocean.

"Then we are going to BCO him," Silvio explained.

"BCO? What's that?"

Silvio leans in and whispers.

"*Barrel-Cement-Ocean.*"

The way the plan all came together so fast seemed like fate. It was unclear at that point in my mind if Uncle Frank played a role in my girl's death that day, but I didn't care anymore. Both Silvio and myself were like primal beasts, totally beside ourselves. My mind was going in slow motion, rewind and fast forward all at the same time. Part of me thought it was – hoping it was all a nightmare that I would soon wake out of.

As the evening became night, the plan went as smoothly as a ticking clock, including Uncle Frank's movements that night. Rosita watched my daughter back in Dumbo.

Uncle Frank looked almost joyful as he walked out of the restaurant that evening. He stumbled to the park. Silvio and as his goon squad waited for the right moment to pounce and quickly muscled him over to the rocks by the water and on to the boat.

Frank was tied, gagged and tossed on the floor where he laid in a small pool of water. We met the fishing vessel out past the Statue of Liberty, where we quickly switched boats. On board, another crew member, who looked Columbian, poured a bag of dry cement in a large blue plastic barrel.

Everybody, Silvio and myself included, worked Frankie over as we went out to sea. The smell of the salty air combined with the smell of blood wafted around the boat. Frank begged in mumbles to stop, which inspired Silvio to smash his ankles with a hammer.

The Colombians took the hammer from Silvio and demonstrated a few tricks from back home on Frank that involved fingernail smashing.

We continued east, way out into the Atlantic. Immediately after water was poured and stirred into the cement mix, Frank was dumped into the barrel feet first. They put more cement mix over him and then more water until only his head and neck stuck out of the cement. Frank was mumbling under the duct tape over his mouth, which everyone ignored. Over Frank's muted screams I listened to President Barack Obama address the nation on a small short-wave radio, and announced the U.S. Military would not attack Syria's dictator, Bashar Hafez al-Assad, after all for gassing innocent civilians – including many women and children – indiscriminately with chemical agents.

Soon it was time.

Silvio pulled off the tape. Frank was hysterical, trembling under the cement and blood.

"You know the more you fucking cry and beg, the more I'm going to torture you Frankie. So just shut the fuck up," Silvio said.

"Silvio, just hear me out..." Frankie said.

"I gotta hand to you Frankie, I would have never guessed it was you who robbed me over and over all these years. And the things you did to my sister, I woulda said 'no way, not Uncle Frank,' he is my blood, he is family. Uncle Frank is ol' school, he would never double-cross family, right Frankie? No, Uncle Frank knows that at the end of the day all you got in the world is family," Silvio said.

"Right Uncle Frankie?" Sivlio said.

"Sil...." Frank begged.

"SHUT THE FUCK UP!" Silvio bellowed.

Silvio punched Franks head a few times, which shut him up once his jaw broke.

"See this guy here," Silvio points to me, "he lived in the woods for four fucking years because of you," Silvio said. "He is writing a book about all this, so your kids and grandkids will know what fucking lowlife scumbag you were."

"He went to college with that other writer, who wrote *American Psycho*. What's his name Kunta?" Silvio asked.

"Brett Easton Ellis," I reply.

"Yeah, that guy," Silvio informed Frankie.

"We didn't go to school together, we went to the same school," I corrected Silvio.

"Shut the fuck up," Silvio said quietly.

"*American Psycho*, I got to be honest, it's one of the few books I actually fucking read. It sucked, sucked bad! Except for the violent parts. That shit was fucking awesome. There is this one scene where the American Psycho sets this chick's eyeballs on fire with a lighter. Fucking incredible! You would love it Frankie, wouldn't you? Isn't that what you're into Frankie, hurting little girls?"

Silvio looked down and pulled out pack of Nat Sherman's.

"Knowing you Uncle Frankie, I bet all you can think about besides saving you fat pathetic ass, is can you get smoke and I guess under the circumstances you are entitled to one, right?" Silvio said.

Silvio lights a cigarette and places it in Frank's mouth. Silvio then hands out cigarettes to his crew and myself. We all smoke quietly as the boat bops around the water. Frank's cigarette is trembling in his mouth.

Frank tried to talk.

"Do you really think their is *anything* you can say to me that would stop what I'm are about to do?" Silvio interrupts.

Silvio put out his cigarette in Frank's eye.

Frank screamed as loud as humanly possible, his little head bounced all around like a toy.

"Come on guys, put them out, we got work to do," Silvio said gesturing over at Frank's head to be used as an ashtray.

One by one cigarettes were put out on Frank's face, as bloodcurdling screams echoed over the Atlantic.

Silvio asked a Columbian if the cement had fully dried. He nodded yes.

"Alright lets cut the bullshit and get this over with," Silvio orders. The crew picked up the barrel and brought it to the back of the boat.

The barrel was put over the side of the boat and on a small platform attached to the back of the boat just above the waterline.

Silvio grabbed a small container of thermite powder the Colombians had given him and poured it over Frank's head.

Frank begged Silvio to stop. Silvio told Frank that "Regina will be taking over your operations on the Upper West Side."

"And this for what you did to her," Silvio said to Frank.

Silvio picked up the cigarette Frank dropped on the floor and flicked it into Frank's face. When that didn't ignite his uncle's head, Silvio took a butane torch and set the thermite powder on Frank's dome ablaze. The flesh burst into a ball of flames and danced with each of Frank's jerking motions. Silvio fired a .45-caliber into the air twice before he kicked the barrel into the Atlantic. Silvio fired into the water as Frank's head still burned and the barrel plummeted downward. You could see Franks head jerking around as he sunk downward, until he was so far down the flame was just a little dot. Then finally, the ocean went dark. One of the Colombians put his hand on Silvio's shoulder and asked him to stop firing.

We drank a bottle of whiskey on the way home. No one said a word, except for Silvio, who said he "got a tip that Pope Francis would be assassinated, probably in America," by the Italian Cosa Nostra "for fucking (reforming) with the Vatican Bank."

I opened my apartment door in Dumbo, which smelled of rice and beans. Rosita and my daughter had conked out on the sofa to

Hellboy cartoons. When the sun rose, I woke my daughter up and took her down to the annual 9/11 memorial at "ground zero". It was the first time a memorial would be held as the new One World Trade Center skyscraper stood externally complete above the 9/11 memorial site.

After the memorial, I took my daughter to Lombardi's pizza on Spring street in Little Italy, credited with being the first pizza shop in America. We cabbed over to St. Brigit's Church on the Lower East Side and lit a candle for my daughter's dead mother. We cabbed to Grand Central and trained up to

Lombardi's Pizza, Little Italy, New York.

the Harlem Line to Scarsdale. I dug out my money in the woods and cabbed to a nearby used car dealership. I bought a used black PT-Cruiser, which they registered for me at the dealership with the Dumbo address. We drove off the lot and headed back to Dumbo.

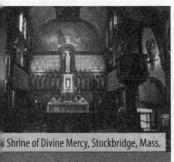

Shrine of Divine Mercy, Stockbridge, Mass.

e of Saint Kateri Tekakwitha, Fonda, NY.

After I packed my dog and our stuff in the car, I drove into Chinatown for one last bag of take out. Then we were off to the Berkshires, where got a room at the Red Lion Inn, in Stockbridge, Massachusetts. The next morning we walked up to the National Shrine of Divine Mercy about block away for a morning mass. After mass, we drove to Fonda, New York, to the shrine of Saint Keteri Takiwitha and went to another afternoon mass.

From there I drove until we reached Milan, Ohio. From Baraboo Wisconsin to Salem, South Dakota and then straight to Butte, Montana, where I met the owner of a cabin I rented adjacent to Glacier National Park for the winter.

The next morning we drove into town and stopped at Evel Knievel's grave. I looked up at the peaks of the Continental Divide which towered over Butte entirely and saw a 90 foot statue of the Virgin Mary watching over us all. We snaked through the Divide to Glacier National Park, truly one of the most beautiful places in the world. We parked the car and walked a mile into the woods. There the cabin was, with only a spring nearby for water, a gas-powered generator for electricity and a wood stove for heat.

It was a long, lonely, cold winter, but one that I needed in order to heal from all that unfolded so quickly in my life. Sitting out there in the deep silence of the Montana wilderness, it was hard to believe it all actually happened.

Evel Knievel's grave, engraved with a drawing of the Skycycle X2.

Lady Of The Rockies, Butte, Montana. Built in 1985 – one year before Burning Man – it honors women of all religions.

Rogers' cabin, Glacier National Park, Montana.

On Christmas Eve, we drove into town to get a few things for the holidays. I stopped by the post office and there was some packages waiting for us from family and friends.

The next morning we opened our presents under the tree. One of them was from Silvio, a CD of traditional Sicilian Mafia music along with the Godfather Trilogy on DVD.

Later that evening after dinner, I went outside and cranked up the generator as a heavy snow began to fall. I put one of the disks in my laptop and the music began.

My daughter ran from her room into the living room and started to dance.

"This is nice," she said innocently while whirling around the cabin floor. The fire's light and shadows from the stove flickered across her red, flannel nightgown.

I lifted up the package that Silvio sent to throw it into the wood stove but, felt more weight inside. I looked under the bubble wrap and saw a vacuum sealed QP of purplish green bud, and another gift that was wrapped in a oak box that had my daughters name written across the top. I handed it to her, and she proceeded to rip off the wrapping paper.

Inside was Pasquale's over the top gold, diamond encrusted chain of the Lady of Guadalupe, looking like it had been just freshly polished. I had not seen it in twenty years, since we all tripped on mushrooms in Vermont. My daughter put the chain around

Our Lady of Guadalupe

her neck, and started to dance again. I looked down at the Lady on the chain – which would have made Floyd Mayweather Jr. envious – and "She" danced in the light of burning white birch blazing in the stove. Large blinding bright diamonds – set exactly on the Virgin Mary's cloak where the stars in the cosmos were accurately placed astrologically on the original image – illuminated through the light created by the fire.

I took a glass pipe I had from the living room and stuffed it with bud, opened the front door of the cabin and stepped outside onto the front porch. The snow drifted downward as I lit up and memories from the last twenty years flashed though my mind.

As the music echoed from my laptop from inside, I imagined what happened to Silvio back in New York after I took off out west. Having bumped off the family patriarch, Silvio usurped the Eboli clan's throne in Little Italy during the Feast of San Gennaro.

After all this time Silvio would finally be the Boss of the Eboli family and it will be his ring people will kiss all over New York City.

Feast of San Gennaro, Little Italy, New York City.